CRIMES
BY
BHARAT KI LAXMI

WARNING TO BACHELORS

RUDOLPH DSOUZA

Made with ♡ on the Notion Press Platform

www.notionpress.com

Legal Disclaimer

This book is intended for informational and educational purposes only. It does not constitute legal advice. Readers are advised to consult with legal professionals for specific guidance on legal matters.

For permissions, inquiries, or media requests, please contact:

Printed in India

Dedication

To my two precious Gems,
Samuel and Sophia;

Whose laughter echoes in my heart,
Who bring joy even in silence,
Though miles and circumstances keep us apart.

May this book be a bridge where my love for you flows freely,
A testament to the unbreakable bond we share,
Through the trials and tribulations imposed by the tides of life,
You are forever in my thoughts, my dreams, in my prayers and my every heartbeat.

I yearn for the day when love conquers distance,
When we can play, talk, and simply be together again.
Until then, know this — you are the light that guides me,
And I carry you with me, today and always.

With all my love,

Dad

Acknowledgments

This book is dedicated to the countless men who became victims of their wives' greed, biased laws, and a prejudiced society. It honours those who lost their lives, those driven to take their own in despair, and those silenced by a system that betrayed them. Your struggles will not be forgotten. I bow my head to the voiceless men who suffered in silence—unheard, unseen, and unacknowledged. This book is for them, the silent sufferers who bore their pain alone, pushed to the brink by circumstances beyond their control and a system that failed to protect them.

I also extend my deepest gratitude to all the members of ***MyNation Hope Foundation***, who stand as a beacon of hope and support for those battling this injustice. Your courage, resilience, and unwavering commitment to justice inspire this work.

Special thanks to Aman Kumar from Patna a life member of *MyNation Hope Foundation* for his dedication over the last four years in tweeting the thread titled **#CrimesByIndianWomen**

Let the unheard be heard.

With gratitude,

RUDOLPH DSOUZA

Author's Note

In writing ***Crimes by Bharat Ki Laxmi***, I felt compelled to address a harsh reality that is often ignored due to deep-rooted societal biases. I felt a responsibility to confront a narrative that is often left unchallenged. Our society, along with its legal systems and institutions, has long operated under the assumption that women are inherently victims and men are their oppressors. While it is undeniable that some women face injustices and harassment, it is equally true that not all women are virtuous simply by virtue of their gender. There exists a darker reality where many women exploit these deeply ingrained biases, committing acts of harassment, abuse, and even murder—often escaping accountability due to laws that are overwhelmingly tilted in their favor.

The principle that "crime has no gender" emphasizes that criminal behavior should be judged solely based on the act committed, not the gender of the perpetrator. Justice must be blind to gender bias— whether the offender is male, female, or of any other identity, the punishment should be proportionate to the severity of the crime, not influenced by societal stereotypes or selective sympathy.

Gender-biased laws or enforcement dilute the very essence of justice and can lead to misuse, false

accusations, or denial of justice to real victims.
Equal treatment under the law is a cornerstone of a
fair legal system. Therefore, punishment should be
as per the crime—not as per gender.

This book is not an attack on women, nor an
indictment of women as a whole but a call for
balance and fairness in the way we perceive justice.
It seeks to bring balance to the conversation,
acknowledging that crime and cruelty are not bound
by gender. By shedding light on these difficult truths,
I hope to encourage a more honest dialogue about
justice—one that isn't limited by societal
preconceptions, but rather grounded in fairness for
all.

Through this work, I hope to initiate a much-needed
dialogue about gender-neutral laws and a justice
system that truly serves everyone, regardless of
gender.

Disclaimer: We do not endorse or promote any
crimes or methods used by women to harm or kill
their husbands; this content is provided strictly for
informational purposes only.

Table of Contents

Preface

The biological distinctions between men and women have been a cornerstone of human evolution, shaping physical and psychological traits that influence behavior, capabilities, and societal roles. While these differences exist, modern advancements have enabled both sexes to perform most tasks interchangeably, challenging traditional gender roles. However, in India, a complex interplay of legal frameworks, societal norms, and media portrayal has created a narrative that often positions women as victims of men, overshadowing instances of male victimization. Women's organizations and government ministries amplify this narrative, promoting laws and schemes exclusively for women, while men face harsher punishments and receive little legal or social support.

In today's skewed socio-legal climate, many women exploit the shield of victimhood to escape accountability for their actions. By shedding tears and playing the "hapless woman" victim card, they manipulate public sympathy and dodge consequences, even for serious crimes. The moment they are questioned or confronted, the blame is swiftly shifted to patriarchy—a convenient scapegoat that instantly silences scrutiny. This tactic not only undermines real victims but also turns the justice system into a tool of gender-based bias, where men are presumed guilty and women are presumed innocent, no matter the evidence.

If we are to move toward a truly just and equal society, we must discard the myth that gender

defines morality or criminality. A woman, like a man,
is fully capable of making decisions—good or evil.
Laws must be gender-neutral, and society must learn
to support all victims, regardless of the perpetrator's
gender. This means better legal recognition of female-
perpetrated crimes, more resources for male victims,
and a shift in public discourse to acknowledge that
violence knows no gender.

Recognizing that women can rape and murder men is
not about vilifying women—it is about acknowledging
the full spectrum of human behavior. Just as men
must be held accountable for their actions, so must
women. True equality does not come from shielding
one gender from scrutiny but from applying justice
evenly and compassionately across all cases. By
facing these uncomfortable truths, society can better
protect its citizens—regardless of sex—and ensure
that every victim has a voice.

In a society where the narrative often paints women
solely as victims, *Crimes by Bharat ki Laxmi* dares to
uncover the other side of the story - one that is rarely
acknowledged and often deliberately ignored. *Crimes
by Bharat ki Laxmi* is not an attack on womanhood -
it is a call for truth, balance, and justice for all,
regardless of gender.

RUDOLPH DSOUZA
27/05/2025

Introduction

The question of whether men can do everything women can—and vice versa—must be answered in layers. In most cognitive and professional tasks, men and women are equally capable. Women have proven themselves in science, politics, combat, and industry, just as men have succeeded in nursing, teaching, and caregiving.

However, there are biological tasks that cannot be swapped: men cannot bear children, and women do not produce sperm. Even in physical labor, although women can train and develop strength, men generally have a natural advantage due to muscle mass and testosterone levels. In contrast, women often endure long-term physical stress (like childbirth and breastfeeding) more effectively than men.

Men and women differ biologically, but these differences do not preclude them from performing most tasks interchangeably. However, India's legal and social systems disproportionately favor women, driven by a narrative of female victimization that overshadows male suffering. Laws like the PWDVA and Section 498A protect women but exclude men, while women offenders often receive leniency. Media underreporting of crimes against men, such as the estimated 600+ annual husband murders, compounds this bias, with practices like covering female suspects' faces further skewing perceptions. These disparities violate principles of equality and justice, harming both men and women. By adopting gender-neutral laws, ensuring equal punishment, and promoting balanced media coverage, India can move toward true gender equity, recognizing that both sexes can be victims and perpetrators in the complex tapestry of human relationships.

Women, like men, are capable of committing serious crimes such as rape and murder against men, challenging the societal narrative that positions women solely as victims. Rape, often framed as a male-perpetrated crime, can be perpetrated by women through coercion, manipulation, or physical force, particularly in cases involving intoxication or blackmail. Indian law, however, does not recognize women as perpetrators of rape under Section 375 of the Indian Penal Code, leaving male victims without legal recourse. Studies, such as a 2013 US National Crime Victimization Survey, indicate that 38% of male rape victims report female perpetrators, suggesting a global underreporting of such cases. In India, cultural stigma and lack of legal recognition discourage men from reporting, as society often dismisses or ridicules male victimization. This gap in acknowledgment perpetuates a cycle where women's capacity for sexual violence against men remains invisible, undermining justice for victims.

Similarly, women can and do murder men, with cases often linked to domestic disputes, extramarital affairs, or financial motives. Media reported cases of husbands murdered by wives in India in 2022, estimating over 600+ such murders annually. These crimes, frequently committed by a man's "trusted and beloved" wife, receive minimal media attention, often relegated to obscure corners of newspapers. The alleged recommendation by the Women's Ministry and radical feminist NGOs to suppress reports of crimes committed by women only worsens this injustice, as does the practice of covering female suspects' faces in media while exposing male suspects. This disparity reinforces stereotypes of women as less culpable, allowing female perpetrators to evade scrutiny and accountability, while male victims' suffering is marginalized.

Crimes by Bharat ki Laxmi exposes the dark underbelly of gender-biased legal systems in India, focusing on crimes committed by women that often go unreported or unpunished. Challenging the popular narrative that sees women solely as victims, this bold and unflinching work presents real-life cases, statistical insights, and critical analysis of laws misused and crimes under the guise of women empowerment.

Through meticulous research, real-world case studies, and an unflinching look at ground realities, Mr. Dsouza's study serves as a clarion call for urgent reforms. His work urges society, policymakers, and judicial institutions to recognize that justice must be balanced - that in the pursuit of protecting one group, we must not knowingly destroy another. Only by addressing these silent sufferings can India hope to build a truly fair, equitable, and '**Viksit Bharat**.'

CHAPTER 1

BIOLOGY

The biological differences between men and women have been a subject of fascination, study, and debate for centuries. These differences span physical, physiological, and psychological domains, shaped by millions of years of evolution, genetics, and environmental influences. While men and women share a common humanity, their biological distinctions influence their capabilities, behaviors, and societal roles. This essay explores the key physical and psychological differences between men and women and examines whether tasks traditionally associated with one sex can be performed by the other.

Physical Differences

The most apparent differences between men and women stem from their reproductive roles, driven by sex chromosomes—XX for women and XY for men. These genetic blueprints influence the development of primary and secondary sexual characteristics. Men typically have higher levels of testosterone, which promotes muscle growth, bone density, and body hair, while women have higher estrogen levels, which support reproductive functions, fat distribution, and softer skin.

- **Musculoskeletal System**: On average, men have greater muscle mass and physical strength due to higher testosterone levels. Studies indicate that men possess about 20-30% more muscle mass than women, giving them an advantage in tasks requiring brute strength, such as lifting heavy objects. Women, however, tend to have greater flexibility and endurance in certain contexts, attributed to differences in muscle fiber composition and hormonal profiles.

- **Body Composition**: Women generally have a higher percentage of body fat (20-25% compared to 10-15% in men), which supports reproductive functions like pregnancy and lactation. This fat distribution, often concentrated in the hips and breasts, contrasts with men's tendency to store fat in the abdominal area. These differences influence physical appearance and energy reserves.

- **Reproductive Anatomy**: Men's reproductive system includes testes, which produce sperm, while women's includes ovaries, fallopian tubes, and a uterus, enabling menstruation, pregnancy, and childbirth. These differences dictate unique physiological experiences, such as menopause in women, which has no direct equivalent in men, though aging affects both sexes.

- **Brain Structure**: While male and female brains are largely similar, subtle differences exist. Men's brains are slightly larger on average (about 10%), correlating with body size, but this does not imply superior intelligence. Women tend to have a higher proportion of gray matter (involved in processing), while men have more white matter (involved in connectivity). The corpus callosum, which connects brain hemispheres, is relatively larger in women, potentially enhancing multitasking abilities.

Psychological Differences

Psychological differences between men and women are more controversial, as they are influenced by both biology and environment. Hormones like testosterone and estrogen play a role in shaping behavior, but socialization, culture, and individual variation complicate the picture.

- **Cognitive Abilities**: Research suggests small, average differences in cognitive strengths. Men tend to excel in spatial reasoning tasks, such as navigation or mental rotation of objects, potentially linked to evolutionary roles like hunting. Women often perform better in verbal and emotional intelligence tasks, possibly due to enhanced connectivity in brain regions like the prefrontal cortex. However, these are population-level trends with significant overlap—many women outperform men in spatial tasks, and vice versa.
- **Emotional Expression**: Women are often stereotyped as more emotionally expressive, while men are seen as stoic. Some studies support this, suggesting women may have a slight edge in empathy and emotional recognition, potentially due to estrogen's role in

modulating emotional circuits. Men, influenced by testosterone, may exhibit greater aggression or risk-taking behavior, though these traits vary widely.

- **Mental Health**: Men and women show different vulnerabilities to psychological disorders. Women are more likely to experience depression and anxiety, possibly due to hormonal fluctuations and societal pressures. Men have higher rates of substance abuse and antisocial personality disorders, potentially linked to testosterone and socialization patterns.

Interchangeability of Tasks

The question of whether men and women can perform each other's tasks hinges on the nature of the task and the influence of biology versus training. Historically, tasks were divided along gendered lines—men as hunters or warriors, women as caregivers or gatherers—based on physical differences and reproductive roles. Modern technology and societal shifts, however, have blurred these lines.

- **Physical Tasks**: Many tasks once deemed "male" due to strength requirements, such as construction or firefighting, are now accessible to women through training and technology. For example, women in the military perform roles like combat soldiers, leveraging fitness and equipment to overcome average strength differences. Conversely, men can excel in tasks traditionally associated with women, such as cooking or sewing, which require dexterity and patience rather than brute strength. However, tasks tied to reproductive biology—childbirth for women or sperm production for men—remain exclusive.

- **Cognitive and Emotional Tasks**: Psychological tasks, such as leadership, nurturing, or problem-solving, show no inherent barriers. Men can be empathetic caregivers, just as women can be decisive leaders. Studies of workplace performance show that gender does not predict competence in roles like management or teaching, though biases may influence perceptions. For instance, women CEOs like Indra Nooyi and men in nursing demonstrate that skill, not sex, determines success.

- **Limitations and Considerations**: While most tasks are interchangeable with training, some biological constraints persist. For example, women's higher endurance in certain contexts (e.g., ultra-marathon running) doesn't negate men's average advantage in explosive strength sports like weightlifting. Similarly, men cannot breastfeed, though they can bottle-feed or provide other forms of infant care. Psychological differences, like risk tolerance, may influence task preferences but not capability.

Conclusion

Men and women differ physically and psychologically due to genetic, hormonal, and evolutionary factors. These differences—muscle mass, reproductive anatomy, brain structure, and behavioral tendencies—reflect adaptations to historical roles but do not rigidly dictate modern capabilities. With training, technology, and societal support, men and women can perform nearly all tasks traditionally associated with the other sex, except those tied directly to reproductive biology. The overlap in abilities, coupled with individual variation, underscores that competence transcends gender. As society continues to evolve, embracing this interchangeability fosters equality and maximizes human potential, allowing both men and women to thrive in diverse roles.

CHAPTER 2

CRIME AND PUNISHMENT

In discussions about crime and justice, particularly those involving sexual violence or homicide, the narrative often focuses on men as perpetrators and women as victims. This framing, while statistically grounded to some degree, overlooks an uncomfortable but critical truth: women, too, are capable of committing rape and murder. The reluctance of society, law enforcement, and even media to acknowledge this reality perpetuates a gender-biased approach to justice, which harms both male victims and the integrity of the legal system.

Female-Perpetrated Rape: The Hidden Crime

Rape, by its legal and social definition, has long been associated with male aggression. For years, laws in many countries did not even consider that a woman could rape a man—either due to biological assumptions or gender stereotypes. However, as definitions evolve, particularly those recognizing non-consensual sexual acts involving coercion, manipulation, or force beyond penetration, the possibility of women as perpetrators becomes not just possible, but evident.

Studies and anecdotal accounts show that men can and do experience sexual violence at the hands of women. This can include cases where women exploit intoxicated, unconscious, or emotionally vulnerable men, or manipulate situations (especially in positions of power) to engage in unwanted sexual acts. Male victims often face unique hurdles: societal disbelief, mockery, and a lack of support services. Many do not report the abuse due to shame or fear of being disbelieved. This cultural blind spot leaves a category of sexual violence largely ignored.

Murders by Women: An Inconvenient Truth

When a woman kills a man, it is often interpreted through a lens of selfdefence or desperation. While such scenarios exist and must be compassionately examined, the idea that women are incapable of premeditated, cold-blooded murder is false. There are numerous high-profile and lesser-known cases worldwide where women have murdered men due to Extra-marital Affairs, jealousy, financial gain, revenge, or manipulation. Some use indirect methods—such as Trap other man/Lover to kill, make like accident, poisoning, false accusations leading to mob violence, or legal system abuse—making their actions harder to detect or prove.

In intimate partner violence (IPV), women are not always the victims. Many men suffer physical and emotional abuse in silence, fearing disbelief or social humiliation. In extreme cases, this abuse escalates into homicide. Moreover, some women have been known to provoke or falsely accuse men to cover up their crimes or avoid accountability. Ignoring these realities not only victimizes innocent men but also distorts the true dynamics of violence in society.

Legal and Social Bias

The justice system often operates under a chivalrous bias when it comes to female offenders. Women who commit serious crimes frequently receive lighter sentences or are portrayed sympathetically by media, especially if they are mothers or victims of past abuse. While compassion has its place, justice must remain balanced. Conversely, male victims are often questioned more harshly or mocked for "allowing" a woman to harm them, especially in cases of sexual violence. These double standards undermine the principle of gender-neutral justice.

The notion that "women can rape too and murder a man" highlights a critical disparity in the Indian legal system, where women often face leniency or inadequate legal scrutiny compared to men for similar crimes. This "stepmother policy," as you describe it, stems from a combination of cultural biases, legislative frameworks, and societal narratives that prioritize women as victims and men as perpetrators. Below, I explore why this disparity exists, focusing on the legal treatment of rape and murder, its societal roots, and the consequences of this biased approach.

Legal Disparities in Handling Rape and Murder

Rape Laws

Indian law, specifically Section 375 of the Indian Penal Code (IPC), defines rape as an act committed by a man against a woman, explicitly excluding women as perpetrators or men as victims of rape.

This gender-specific framing ignores cases where women coerce, manipulate, or physically force men into sexual acts, such as through blackmail, intoxication, or threats. For instance, a woman compelling a man to engage in sexual activity under duress—common in cases involving false promises of marriage or financial extortion—does not qualify as rape under Indian law. The only provision addressing male victimization, Section 377 (unnatural offenses), is narrowly applied and rarely used against women perpetrators. In contrast, men accused of rape face stringent punishments, including a minimum of seven years' imprisonment, with little room for leniency.

This legal gap is stark when compared to global standards. Studies like the 2013 US National Crime Victimization Survey reveal that 38% of male rape victims report female perpetrators, indicating that women's capacity for sexual violence is not negligible. In India, Public Interest Litigations (PILs) advocating for gender-neutral rape laws, such as one filed in 2016, have been opposed by women's organizations arguing that such changes would dilute protections for female victims. This resistance, coupled with legislative inaction, ensures that male victims of female-perpetrated rape lack legal recourse, reinforcing the perception that women cannot commit such crimes.

Murder Laws

In cases of murder, Indian law under Section 302 of the IPC applies equally to both genders, prescribing life imprisonment or the death penalty. However, judicial discretion and societal biases often result in leniency for women. Women convicted of murdering men, particularly husbands, may receive lighter sentences or suspended terms, especially if the defense cites provocation, abuse, or emotional distress. For example, a 2018 case in Maharashtra saw a woman convicted of killing her husband receive a reduced sentence after claiming domestic abuse, despite contested evidence. Men, conversely, rarely benefit from such leniency when invoking provocation, facing harsher penalties for equivalent crimes.

Data on husband murders by wives, while underreported, is alarming. A media report of such cases in 2022, estimating over 600 annually, often linked to extramarital affairs or financial motives. Yet, these cases receive minimal media attention, and women perpetrators are often portrayed sympathetically or shielded from public scrutiny, with their faces covered in media coverage unlike male suspects. The United Nations Office on Drugs and Crime notes that women globally receive lighter sentences due to paternalistic judicial attitudes, a trend evident in India where women are seen as less threatening or culpable.

Reasons for the "Stepmother Policy"

The preferential treatment of women in Indian law and society arises from a complex interplay of historical, cultural, and political factors:

Patriarchal Legacy and Victim Narrative: India's patriarchal history has paradoxically created a legal pendulum swing favouring women. Feminist movements in the 1980s, responding to rampant dowry deaths and sexual violence, successfully lobbied for women-centric laws like the Protection of Women from Domestic Violence Act (PWDVA) and Section 498A (anti-dowry cruelty). These laws, while addressing genuine issues, entrenched the narrative that women are perpetual victims of male oppression. This narrative, amplified by women's organizations and the Ministry of Women and Child Development, overlooks male victimization, framing men as aggressors even when they are victims of rape or murder.

Cultural Stereotypes: Indian society views women as inherently nurturing and less violent, aligning with traditional roles as mothers and caregivers. This stereotype influences judges, police, and media, who may perceive women's crimes as anomalies driven by external factors like abuse or coercion. A Times of India article noted that society "laughs" at men claiming rape or abuse, discouraging them from seeking justice.

Political and Feminist Advocacy: Women's organizations wield significant influence, advocating for policies that protect women while dismissing male issues. The Ministry of Women and Child Development, established to promote women's welfare, focuses exclusively on female-centric schemes like the Nirbhaya Fund and Beti Bachao

Beti Padhao, with no equivalent for men. Allegations that the ministry recommended suppressing women's crimes in media, though unverified, align with biased narratives. Feminist opposition to gender-neutral laws, as seen in the 2016 PIL, prioritizes female protections over equitable justice, perpetuating the legal double standard.

Judicial Paternalism: Indian courts often adopt a paternalistic view, treating women as vulnerable and in need of protection. This leads to lighter sentences or acquittals for women, particularly in domestic violence or murder cases where emotional or abusive contexts are cited. The Supreme Court has acknowledged misuse of laws like Section 498A, where women file false complaints "in the heat of the moment," yet such misuse rarely faces punishment, unlike false accusations by men.

Media Bias: Media plays a pivotal role in shaping public perception, often underreporting or downplaying women's crimes. Husband murders by wives, despite their frequency, are relegated to obscure news sections, while violence against women dominates headlines. The practice of covering female suspects' faces, unlike male suspects, reinforces the notion that women's crimes are less severe. This selective reporting aligns with societal biases and gender bias.

CHAPTER 3

WOMAN VS. MAN

In modern society, the idea of equality has been widely advocated—but ironically, often selectively. One of the most divisive forces operating today is the gender-based narrative pushed by certain political bodies, NGOs, and international organizations. While advocating for women's rights is essential, the approach often taken by women's ministries, feminist NGOs, and even global institutions like UN Women has contributed significantly to gender polarization, often side-lining legitimate issues faced by men.

The issue of gender equality has been a cornerstone of social and political discourse for decades, with various organizations, including women's ministries, non-governmental organizations (NGOs), and international bodies like the United Nations (UN) and UN Women, playing significant roles in shaping policies and public perceptions. While these entities often aim to address systemic inequalities faced by women, their approaches can sometimes exacerbate gender divisions, promote biased laws, and prioritize certain groups over others. This essay explores how these organizations advocate for feminism, how their lobbying efforts influence resource allocation, who benefits from gender-biased laws, and how politicians exploit these dynamics for electoral gains.

The Gender Divide: Roots and Manifestations

The gender divide refers to the societal, economic, and political disparities between men and women, often rooted in historical power imbalances, cultural norms, and institutional structures. While women have historically faced discrimination in areas such as education, employment, and political representation, men also encounter challenges, including higher workplace mortality rates, shorter life expectancies, and biases in family court systems. The divide is perpetuated when advocacy focuses exclusively on one gender's issues, ignoring the interconnected nature of societal problems.

Feminist movements, particularly since the 1970s, have gained momentum globally, with milestones like the UN's International Women's Year (1975) and the Beijing Declaration (1995) marking significant steps toward gender equality. However, some feminist approaches have been criticized for framing gender issues as a zero-sum game, where advancing women's rights is perceived to come at the expense of men's. This has led to a polarized discourse, where men's rights groups argue that their concerns—such as mental health, homelessness, or parental rights— are side-lined by feminist-dominated advocacy.

The Influence of International Bodies

Women's ministries, NGOs, and international organizations like UN Women are central to promoting feminist agendas. UN Women, established in 2010, consolidates efforts to advance gender equality by supporting member states in designing gender-responsive policies and budgets. It focuses on areas like women's political participation, economic empowerment, and ending violence against women. Similarly, NGOs such as the European Women's Lobby (EWL) and the National Organization for Women (NOW) advocate for women's rights through lobbying, litigation, and public campaigns.

These organizations often collaborate with governments to implement gender-specific programs, such as gender-responsive budgeting, which ensures that public funds address women's needs. For instance, UN Women has developed methodologies to track allocations for gender equality, influencing fiscal policies in numerous countries. While these efforts aim to rectify historical disadvantages, they can inadvertently prioritize women's issues over universal challenges. For example, social protection systems like maternity leave or women-focused cash transfers are often emphasized, while issues like men's mental health or workplace safety receive less attention.

Organizations like the United Nations and its entity UN Women play a major role in shaping global gender policy. However, their agenda is often one-sided. UN Women, in particular, promotes feminism globally but largely ignores issues such as male suicide, domestic abuse against men, parental alienation, false accusations, and the lack of male-centric health or legal support systems.

International funding is frequently tied to gender-specific programs aimed solely at women, while any demand for male inclusion is dismissed or

underfunded. This has a trickle-down effect:
governments avoid setting up male welfare programs
or men's commissions for fear of losing international
goodwill or financial aid.

The Role of Women's Ministries and NGOs

Across many countries, dedicated women's
ministries have been established with the stated aim
of promoting women's welfare. However, in practice,
these institutions often focus exclusively on female
issues while completely ignoring men's rights and
suffering. This selective focus has institutionalized
gender favoritism. Rather than promoting gender-
neutral policies that address the issues of all
citizens, these ministries often lobby for female-
centric laws, creating an imbalance in policy
frameworks.

Similarly, a large number of women's NGOs thrive on
a narrative of victimhood. Their funding, influence,
and survival depend on maintaining the perception
that women are always victims and men are always
perpetrators. These NGOs frequently use skewed
data and anecdotal evidence to push for laws that
favor one gender, leading to legal frameworks that
are biased and easily misused. This not only affects
innocent men but also real female victims who get
lost in a system flooded with false cases.

Moreover, some NGOs and ministries have been
criticized for lobbying for laws that appear gender-
biased. In countries like India, laws such as Section
498A of the Indian Penal Code, intended to protect

women from domestic violence, have been misused
in some cases to falsely implicate men, leading to
calls for reform from men's rights groups. Similarly,
in Western nations, family court biases favoring
women in custody disputes have sparked debates
about fairness. These laws, often championed by
feminist organizations, can strain gender relations
when perceived as one-sided.

Blocking Resources for Shared Challenges

A significant critique of feminist advocacy is its
potential to divert resources from programs that
benefit both genders. For instance, funding for
women's shelters or gender-based violence initiatives
is often prioritized over universal anti-violence
programs. In 2021-2022, funding for women's rights
organizations dropped significantly, yet the focus
remained on women-specific issues rather than
broader societal challenges like poverty or healthcare
access, which affect both men and women.

International bodies like UN Women emphasize
gender-specific interventions, such as women's
economic empowerment, but rarely address issues
like male homelessness or suicide, which are
statistically significant. This selective focus can
create a perception that men's struggles are less
valid, fueling resentment and further entrenching the
gender divide. In some cases, NGOs have opposed
gender-neutral policies, arguing that they dilute the
focus on women's issues. For example, efforts to
make domestic violence laws gender-neutral in
certain countries have faced resistance from feminist

groups, who argue that women are disproportionately affected and thus deserve exclusive protections.

Who Profits from Gender-Biased Laws?

Gender-biased laws create entire ecosystems of beneficiaries. Legal professionals, NGO workers, counselling centers, and even certain media outlets profit from the sensationalism and cases that arise from these laws. Laws that allow arrests without investigation, such as certain misuse-prone provisions related to domestic violence or dowry harassment, are often exploited for extortion or personal vendettas. The legal machinery becomes a weapon, not a shield.

Moreover, government grants and foreign aid often come with gender tags. This incentivizes institutions to project women as perpetual victims in need of constant support, thereby ensuring the flow of funds. In contrast, there's hardly any lobbying for male-specific funds or mental health resources for men, despite alarming suicide and depression statistics.

Gender-biased laws, often the result of intense lobbying by feminist organizations, can benefit specific groups while disadvantaging others. Women, particularly those in vulnerable situations, may gain access to legal protections, financial support, or social services. For instance, laws mandating equal pay or quotas for women in politics have increased female representation and economic participation in countries like Iceland and Rwanda.

However, these laws can also be exploited. In some cases, individuals misuse legal provisions for personal gain, such as false allegations in domestic violence cases or leveraging custody biases for financial settlements. Lawyers and advocacy groups may profit by representing clients in such disputes, creating a cottage industry around gender-related litigation. Additionally, NGOs and ministries sustain their relevance and funding by perpetuating narratives of gender oppression, sometimes exaggerating issues to secure grants or public support.

Politicians and policymakers also benefit by aligning with feminist causes, which appeal to a significant voter base. By championing women's rights, they gain moral credibility and political capital, even if their policies fail to address broader societal inequities.

Politics and the Gender Vote Bank

Politicians are not innocent bystanders in this gender divide. Many political parties exploit gender narratives for electoral gains. By positioning themselves as "protectors of women," they attract votes and goodwill, especially from female constituencies. Even when there is clear evidence of misuse of gender-biased laws, political leaders hesitate to address the issue, fearing backlash or loss of votes.

Politicians exploit gender issues as a vote bank strategy, capitalizing on the emotional and social resonance of women's rights. Women represent half the global population, making them a powerful electoral demographic. By endorsing feminist policies, politicians can appeal to women voters and progressive constituencies. For example, in countries like Brazil and Morocco, governments have highlighted women's political participation to signal progressive credentials, even when systemic issues like poverty remain unaddressed.

Gender-biased laws and programs are often framed as moral imperatives, making opposition politically risky. Politicians may support quotas, subsidies, or women-specific welfare schemes to secure votes, even if these measures strain public budgets or overlook men's needs. In India, for instance, political parties frequently promise women-centric schemes—like free transport or cash transfers—during elections, knowing they resonate with female voters. This strategy can deepen the gender divide by reinforcing the notion that women's issues are separate from men's, rather than part of a shared societal framework.

Moreover, politicians benefit from the advocacy of NGOs and international bodies, which provide data, narratives, and moral authority to justify gender-specific policies. The UN's Sustainable Development Goals (SDGs), particularly Goal 5 on gender equality, are often cited by politicians to align domestic policies with global standards, enhancing their international reputation.

This vote-bank politics leads to a lack of political will to introduce gender-neutral laws or create men's commissions. Any such move is quickly labeled as "anti-women" by influential NGOs and media, stifling any balanced discourse.

Critical Examination and Moving Forward

While feminist advocacy has achieved significant progress, such as increased women's representation and legal protections, its current trajectory risks alienating men and perpetuating division. The focus on women-specific issues, often at the expense of universal challenges, can create a zero-sum perception, where one gender's gain is another's loss. This is exacerbated by lobbying for laws that, while well-intentioned, may lack nuance or fairness in implementation.

To bridge the gender divide, advocacy must adopt a more inclusive approach. Policies should address shared challenges—like poverty, mental health, and violence—without prioritizing one gender. Gender-neutral laws, coupled with robust enforcement and public education, could reduce misuse and foster trust. NGOs and international bodies should diversify their focus, acknowledging men's issues alongside women's to create a balanced narrative. Politicians, meanwhile, must resist the temptation to exploit gender for votes, instead promoting policies that unite rather than divide.

Conclusion

The gender divide is a complex issue, amplified by the advocacy of women's ministries, NGOs, and international bodies like UN Women, which often prioritize feminist goals over inclusive solutions. While their efforts have advanced women's rights, they can also block resources for shared challenges and promote biased laws that strain gender relations. Those who benefit—whether individuals exploiting legal loopholes, advocacy groups securing funding, or politicians chasing votes—often do so at the cost of societal cohesion. A critical re-examination of these dynamics is essential to foster policies that uplift all, ensuring that gender equality becomes a unifying force rather than a divisive one.

CHAPTER 4

WARNING TO BACHELORS

In India today, being a bachelor or a married man has become a matter of fear and uncertainty—not because of personal shortcomings, but because of a deeply flawed legal system that overwhelmingly favors women in matrimonial and gender-related disputes. Laws created with good intentions to protect women from abuse are being misused rampantly, and the consequences are devastating for innocent men and their families.

What was once supposed to be the sacred institution of marriage has now become a potential legal trap. The moment a man enters into a marriage in India, he becomes vulnerable to a host of one-sided laws that can ruin his life, reputation, finances, and future—often without even a shred of evidence.

In contemporary India, the institution of marriage, traditionally viewed as a sacred union, has become a source of apprehension for many bachelors due to the prevalence of gender-biased laws and their potential for misuse. Laws such as Section 498A of the Indian Penal Code, the Domestic Violence Act (DVA), and rape provisions, while designed to protect women, are often criticized for their one-sided application, leaving men and their families vulnerable to false accusations. With minimal legal recourse, prolonged judicial processes, and severe financial and emotional consequences, these laws have created a climate of fear among men contemplating marriage. This essay explores why bachelors in India have reason to be cautious, the lack of protective laws for men, the devastating impact of false allegations, and the urgent need to warn prospective grooms about the risks of becoming victims of what some term "legal terrorism."

The Dangers of Women-Centric Laws

India's legal framework includes several provisions aimed at protecting women from abuse and discrimination, reflecting the country's commitment to addressing historical gender inequalities. Section 498A, enacted in 1983, criminalizes cruelty by a husband or his relatives toward a wife, with penalties including up to three years of imprisonment. The Domestic Violence Act of 2005 provides women with protections against physical, emotional, and economic abuse, offering remedies like maintenance and residence orders. Rape laws under Section 375 of the Indian Penal Code have also been strengthened, particularly after high-profile cases, to ensure swift justice for victims.

While these laws are well-intentioned, their implementation often lacks balance. A woman's statement alone can trigger arrests under these provisions, with minimal initial evidence required. Section 498A, for instance, is non-bailable and non-compoundable in many cases, meaning that the accused—often the husband and his family—can be detained without bail until a court hearing. Similarly, the DVA allows women to seek ex-parte orders, which can evict men from their homes or impose financial obligations based solely on allegations. Rape accusations, even if later proven false, can destroy reputations and livelihoods due to their social stigma and legal weight.

The misuse of these laws has been widely documented. According to data from the National Crime Records Bureau (NCRB), a significant percentage of cases under Section 498A are either withdrawn or result in acquittals, suggesting a high rate of false or exaggerated claims. Men's rights groups estimate that up to 70-80% of dowry and domestic violence cases are misused, often as tools for settling personal scores, extracting financial settlements, or gaining leverage in divorce proceedings. The Supreme Court of India has acknowledged this issue, noting in cases like Arnesh Kumar v. State of Bihar (2014) that Section 498A is sometimes used as a weapon rather than a shield, yet reforms remain limited.

In India, laws like Section 498A IPC (Dowry Harassment), Protection of Women from Domestic Violence Act (DV Act), and Sexual Harassment or Rape Laws operate with a presumption of male guilt. A mere statement by a woman—without the need for evidence—can lead to the immediate arrest of the husband, his parents, siblings, and even distant relatives. Entire families have been humiliated, jailed, and socially ostracized based on false complaints.

Once a case is filed, it may take 10–20 years or more to prove one's innocence. Meanwhile, the accused man is dragged from court to court, forced to spend his life savings on legal fees, lose his job due to a damaged reputation, and live under the shadow of false accusations. Ironically, when the truth finally emerges, the false accuser often walks free without any punishment. There is no legal consequence for misusing these laws, leaving a gaping hole in the justice system.

The Absence of Legal Protections for Men

One of the most alarming aspects for bachelors is the lack of legal safeguards for men against false accusations. Unlike women, who have access to dedicated laws and support systems, men have no equivalent protections. There are no specific provisions to address false allegations, harassment by spouses, or extortion through legal means. Men's rights organizations, such as the Save Indian Family Foundation, have long advocated for gender-neutral laws, but such proposals face resistance from feminist groups and policymakers who argue that women's issues remain paramount.

When falsely accused, men and their families face immediate consequences. Arrests under Section 498A often include elderly parents, siblings, and even distant relatives, causing widespread trauma. Bail is difficult to secure, and the presumption of guilt prevails until proven otherwise. The judicial process in India is notoriously slow, with cases dragging on for decades due to backlog—over 40 million pending cases as of 2023, according to the National Judicial Data Grid. During this period, the accused must navigate a labyrinth of lawyers, court hearings, and legal fees, often depleting their life's savings.

Even when innocence is proven, the accuser typically faces no consequences. Indian law rarely penalizes false complaints, as provisions like Section 182 of the Indian Penal Code (false information with intent to cause injury) are seldom enforced in such cases. This impunity emboldens misuse, leaving men with no deterrent against malicious litigation.

Financial and Emotional Toll

The financial repercussions of false allegations are staggering. Men accused under Section 498A or DVA often face exorbitant legal fees, with advocates charging thousands of rupees per hearing. In divorce or maintenance cases, men are frequently ordered to pay hefty alimony, even in short-lived marriages. Under Section 125 of the Code of Criminal Procedure, only women can claim maintenance, regardless of their financial independence, while men have no reciprocal rights. Courts often award significant sums—sometimes 20-50% of a man's income—without rigorous scrutiny of the wife's needs or contributions.

Child custody further compounds the issue. Indian courts overwhelmingly favor mothers, with over 80% of custody cases awarding sole custody to women, according to family court data. Fathers are often reduced to paying child support while being denied visitation rights, leaving them emotionally estranged from their children. The combination of alimony, child support, and legal expenses can bankrupt men, forcing them to liquidate assets or borrow heavily.

The emotional toll is equally devastating. False accusations tarnish reputations, strain family relationships, and lead to social ostracism. Men report high levels of stress, anxiety, and depression, with some resorting to extreme measures. The National Crime Records Bureau reports that men account for over 75% of suicides in India, with marital disputes and legal harassment cited as significant factors. The stigma of being labeled an abuser or rapist, even falsely, can irreparably damage careers and personal lives.

Marriage: A Legal Trap for Men

Many Indian men don't realize that even a one-day-old marriage can entitle the wife to demand huge alimony and monthly maintenance, regardless of her background, education, or earning potential. The law sees only the man's duty to provide, not the woman's responsibility to be fair.

Only women can claim maintenance, not men—even if the wife is abusive, violent, or has deserted the husband. There are no laws to protect men from domestic violence, mental harassment, or emotional trauma inflicted by their wives. The system is not designed to understand a man's suffering.

Fathers Without Rights

In custody battles, women almost always get custody of the child, while the father is reduced to a wallet—

expected to pay child support without getting proper visitation rights. In many cases, fathers are completely alienated from their children and have to fight endlessly just to see them for a few hours in a month—if allowed at all.

This cruel injustice emotionally devastates fathers and children alike. But the law doesn't care. It operates on outdated gender roles, assuming only women can be caregivers and only men can be providers.

The Red Flags for Future Grooms

For bachelors and men planning to marry in India, these are not just legal facts—they are red flags. The blind trust in a relationship is no longer enough. One argument, one disagreement, or one manipulated lic is all it takes to destroy your life. You could become a victim of legal terrorism, imprisoned by a system that listens to one side and silences the other.

For bachelors considering marriage, these realities serve as stark red flags. A marriage lasting even a single day can lead to lifelong financial obligations, with no guarantee of fairness. The ease of filing complaints under women-centric laws, coupled with the lack of accountability for false accusers, creates a power imbalance that leaves men vulnerable. The prospect of losing savings, homes, and access to children deters many from entering matrimony, contributing to declining marriage rates in urban India.

Social media platforms highlight these concerns, with men's rights activists sharing stories of "legal terrorism"—a term coined to describe the systematic misuse of laws to harass men. Posts on social media frequently warn bachelors to conduct thorough background checks, seek prenuptial agreements (though their enforceability in India is limited), or avoid marriage altogether. The sentiment is clear: the risks outweigh the rewards in a system perceived as stacked against men.

A Call for Awareness and Caution

We must wake up and acknowledge the one-sided nature of gender laws in India. Until the laws become gender-neutral and misuse is penalized, men must protect themselves. This includes being cautious before marrying, avoiding emotional or financial dependency, and knowing your legal rights and vulnerabilities.

It is our duty to warn every young man: Do not walk blindly into a system stacked against you. Know the risks. Take precautions. Get legal counselling before marriage. Consider pre-nuptial agreements (though not yet legally binding in India, they help show intent). Protect your family, your future, and your freedom.

Because in today's India, being a man is not enough to prove your innocence. You have to fight for it—often for decades.

Conclusion

The fear among Indian bachelors stems from a legal system that, while aiming to protect women, inadvertently exposes men to exploitation and harassment. Laws like Section 498A, DVA, and rape provisions, combined with the absence of protections for men, create a precarious environment where a single accusation can upend lives. The prolonged judicial process, financial ruin, and emotional devastation faced by the falsely accused underscore the need for caution among those contemplating marriage. As a society, it is our duty to warn bachelors of these risks and advocate for reforms that promote justice for all, ensuring that marriage remains a union of trust rather than a gamble with lifelong consequences. Until such changes are realized, bachelors must tread carefully, armed with knowledge and vigilance, to avoid becoming victims of legal terrorism.

You Could Be the Next Victim

It's easy to believe, "This won't happen to me." But thousands of men, from all walks of life, have said the same before their lives were shattered. If even one woman misuses the law, a man's life becomes a nightmare—and the law won't save him.

Marriage is no longer a risk-free decision for men in India.

Before you say "yes," read, research, and understand the ground realities. Know the laws, the loopholes, and the consequences. Don't step into marriage blindly—step in wisely.

Because once you're trapped, it's not just the end of a relationship—it could be the end of your peace, reputation, and future.

ALL BACHELORS, WE WARNED YOU - THINK BEFORE YOU SAY YES.

CHAPTER 5

HOW WOMEN HARASS?

Harassment in marriage, whether by wives or husbands, often involves emotional, verbal, or psychological tactics that erode trust and well-being. The behaviors listed below — threats of suicide, insulting parents, withholding sex, flaunting affairs, or going out with lovers—can indeed constitute daily harassment when used to control or demean. Adding to this, verbal abuse, financial control, and public humiliation are common tactics that further strain relationships.

Emotional & Psychological Abuse

- Threatening Suicide to manipulate the husband emotionally or force compliance.
- Guilt-tripping or blackmailing over small issues, constantly making the husband feel at fault.
- Silent treatment, ignoring for days to assert control or punishment.
- Public humiliation, shaming the husband in front of family, children, or on social media.
- Using guilt, silent treatment, or mood swings to control the husband's behavior, e.g., ignoring him for days to "punish" minor disagreements.

Verbal & Mental Torture

- Consistent belittling, mocking, name-calling, or abusive language.
- Bringing up past mistakes repeatedly to lower self-esteem.
- Insulting husband's parents, mocking their status, or demanding they be kicked out or sent to old age homes.
- Regular insults, name-calling, or demeaning comments about the husband's appearance, job, or abilities (e.g., "You're useless, you can't even earn enough"). This chips away at self-worth.

Sexual Manipulation

- Withholding sex or affection as a punishment or control tactic. Husband is only to pay her bills, most Indian women treat husband as an ATM.
- Openly having an affair, talking to or meeting a lover in front of the husband.
- Going out with lovers without consent or consideration, sometimes even boasting about it.
- Lack of active participation or emotional connection during intimacy—such as lying motionless, showing indifference, or adopting a 'do it yourself' attitude—can deeply impact a man's emotional well-being. Additionally, making hurtful remarks about his body or performance, like criticizing size or labeling it a 'quickie,' can damage his self-esteem and gradually erode his confidence and libido.

Controlling Behavior

- **Financial control**: demanding full salary, not allowing the husband to manage his own expenses. Stop husband from helping or giving money to his old aged Parents.
- Controlling interactions with friends, family, and even work colleagues.
- Using children to manipulate or threaten, e.g., threatening to take custody or turn them against the father.
- **Excessive Demands**: Setting unrealistic expectations, like demanding constant attention or perfection in household duties, and berating him for falling short.
- Criticizing or mocking the husband in front of friends, family, or on social media to shame him and assert dominance.
- **Gaslighting**: Denying or twisting events to make the husband doubt his reality, e.g., "I never said that, you're imagining things," to avoid accountability.

List of Behaviours and Their Impact:

Threat of Suicide:

Some spouses may threaten self-harm to manipulate or control their partner, creating fear and guilt. For example, saying, "If you don't do what I want, I'll kill myself," can place immense emotional pressure on the husband, forcing compliance to avoid perceived consequences.

Impact: This can lead to anxiety, emotional exhaustion, and a sense of being trapped, as the husband may feel responsible for their spouse's well-being.

Insulting Husband's Parents or Forcing Their Removal:

A spouse might belittle or mock their husband's parents, targeting their character, habits, or role in the family. For instance, making derogatory remarks like, "Your parents are a burden," or pressuring the husband to send them to an old-age home or cut contact.

In some cases, this can escalate to demands that the husband choose between the spouse and his parents, creating familial rifts.

Impact: This undermines the husband's familial bonds, causing guilt, stress, and conflict, especially in Indian households where joint families are common.

Withholding Sex:

Deliberately refusing intimacy as a form of punishment or control, such as saying, "You don't deserve me because you didn't do X," can be a way to manipulate or express resentment.

This differs from personal choice or mutual consent, as it's used to assert power rather than reflect genuine disinterest or comfort levels.

Impact: Can lead to feelings of rejection, inadequacy, or frustration, damaging emotional and physical intimacy in the marriage.

Openly Having an Affair and Talking to Lover in Front of Husband:
Engaging in extramarital relationships and flaunting them, such as taking calls with a lover or discussing the affair openly to taunt the husband, can be a form of emotional abuse. For example, saying, "He's better than you," to provoke or humiliate.

Impact: This erodes trust, self-esteem, and mutual respect, often leaving the husband feeling powerless or betrayed.

Going Out with Lovers Without Husband's Consent:
A spouse might leave the home to meet a romantic partner, disregarding the husband's feelings or the marital commitment, sometimes announcing it to challenge his authority, e.g., "I'm going out, and you can't stop me." As in India husband can't charge wife for Adultery.

Impact: This can cause public humiliation, emotional pain, and a sense of disrespect, particularly in cultures where marital fidelity is highly valued.

Important Notes:
These behaviours, are forms of abuse, and no one—man or woman—should have to live under that stress. If anyone find above said factors in your marriage then you are in Toxic relation.

Men often don't speak up due to social stigma or fear of not being believed. Women can be skilled at fabricating false narratives to elicit sympathy, even when their husband or partner is the actual victim of domestic abuse.

Contextual Notes:

Cultural Factors: In India, societal expectations around marriage, gender roles, and family dynamics can amplify the impact of these behaviours. For instance, insulting parents or pressuring their removal is particularly charged in joint-family setups. However, these issues aren't unique to Indian wives and can occur across cultures or genders.

Escalation to Legal Threats: Mentioned behaviours like threatening false 498A (dowry harassment), DV (domestic violence), or marital rape cases. Even without filing, threatening such actions can be a form of daily harassment, used to intimidate or coerce the husband into compliance due to the fear of legal or social consequences. Same threats sooner than later turn to be tools of Legal terrorism.

Misuse of Laws (Legal Harassment)
- **False cases of**:
- Section 498A IPC (Cruelty by husband or relatives)
- Domestic Violence Act (DV)
- Marital Rape (in states or cases where applicable)
- Threatening arrest, police complaints, or social ruin unless demands are met.
- Using the legal system as leverage in property disputes, divorce settlements, or child custody.

Understanding the Manipulation of Narrative in Abusive Relationships

The Concept: Fabricating a False Narrative

Most Women can be highly manipulative and capable of crafting false stories or exaggerated claims. When a woman does this in the context of a relationship where she is the abuser, the goal may be to:

- Elicit sympathy from friends, family, police, courts, or the public
- Discredit the husband or partner, painting him as violent, negligent, or emotionally abusive
- Preemptively control the narrative, especially in case of separation, divorce, or child custody disputes

How It Happens: Tactics Used

Emotional Storytelling:

- She might tell emotionally charged stories filled with half-truths, selective facts, or fabricated incidents.
- These stories often emphasize her pain, fear, or helplessness—even if she was the aggressor in the situation.

Playing the Victim in Public:

- Crying in front of relatives or friends to gain support.
- Posting emotional content on social media, hinting at being abused, abandoned, or mistreated.
- Portraying the husband as controlling or violent without any proof.

Pre-emptive Legal Strikes:

- Filing false domestic violence, dowry harassment (498A), or marital rape cases to strengthen her position in a separation or custody battle.
- Using these legal complaints to leverage financial settlements or alimony.

Manipulating Social Perception:

- Telling relatives, friends, neighbours or co-workers that she's in a bad marriage, ensuring if conflict arises later, people already side with her.

- Isolating the husband from his support system by accusing his family or friends of mistreating her.
- Telling her family, friends that her husband had an affair and he is neglecting her.

Gaslighting the Husband:
- Denying or minimizing her own abusive behavior.
- Twisting facts to make him question his memory or perception of reality.
- Making him feel guilty for things she initiated (e.g., provoking fights and then crying victim).

Why It's Effective:

- **Societal Bias**: Many people still find it hard to believe that a woman can be abusive or manipulative. Most think Women is victim always.
- **Legal System Limitations**: In India (and many countries), laws like Section 498A, DV Act, and maintenance laws are often heavily tilted in favor of women—and while meant to protect, they can be misused.
- **Emotional Impact**: People naturally want to protect someone who appears vulnerable or in distress.

Impact on the Actual Victim (the Husband)

- He may face character assassination, job loss, social isolation, or even jail time.

- He may become depressed, anxious, or suicidal due to the emotional and social toll.
- He may lose access to children, family, or even his own home.
- Often, his voice is ignored, and his attempts to defend himself are seen as aggression.

Know Your Woman: If You Are in an Abusive Relationship

Abuse doesn't always come with bruises. It can be emotional, psychological, financial, verbal, or even legal. In India, where men have almost no legal protection against domestic abuse, it's critical for men to recognize the red flags before it's too late.

Signs You May Be in an Abusive Relationship:

- She constantly **threatens to file false cases** (498A, DV, dowry, rape).
- She **controls your finances**, isolates you from friends and family.
- She **humiliates or belittles** you publicly or privately.
- She uses **emotional blackmail, self-harm threats**, or your children as weapons.
- She **manipulates** you into guilt or submission, even when you're right.
- She **lies, gaslights**, or twists facts to always be the victim.

- She **refuses to communicate** and uses silent
  treatment as punishment.
- She **controls intimacy** and uses sex as a
  weapon or bargaining chip.

What You Need to Know:

- The law won't believe you unless you have
  proof—start documenting everything.
- In most cases, only the woman is treated as a
  victim.
- Even verbal allegations can ruin your career,
  reputation, and family life.
- There is no legal recourse for abused men, but
  precaution is your best defense.

What You Can Do:

- **Talk to trusted friends** or support groups
  (like men's rights organizations, *MyNation
  Hope Foundation*).
- **Keep records**: messages, calls, threats—
  everything.
- **Avoid retaliation**; stay calm and strategic.
- **Consult a lawyer** early—don't wait until it's
  too late.
- **Plan your exit**, especially if the relationship
  has become legally dangerous.

*You don't have to suffer in silence just because you are a **man**.*

Know your woman. Know the signs. Protect your freedom, peace, and future.

Abuse does not discriminate by gender. As a man, acknowledging that you are in an abusive relationship can be incredibly difficult—especially in a society that expects men to be strong, silent, and invulnerable. But the truth is, being abused does not make you weak. Staying silent does not make you strong. And enduring pain does not prove your masculinity.

If you are experiencing control, manipulation, false accusations, threats, emotional degradation, or physical harm—know that you are not alone, and you are not to blame. Abuse is abuse, regardless of who the victim is.

There is no shame in seeking help. There is courage in choosing to walk away, in protecting your dignity, and in reclaiming your life. Support exists, even if it's harder to find. Stand firm in the truth that your pain is real, and your life matters.

You deserve respect. You deserve peace. You deserve freedom from abuse.

CHAPTER 6

WHY MARRIED INDIAN MEN DIE YOUNG?

The notion that married Indian men die young due to societal pressures, familial obligations, and systemic biases is a complex and sensitive topic. It touches on cultural norms, gender dynamics, legal frameworks, and economic realities in India. While the premise raises valid concerns about the stressors faced by married men, it also risks oversimplification and generalization. This essay explores the factors contributing to the early mortality of married Indian men, focusing on socio-economic pressures, familial expectations, legal vulnerabilities, and health neglect, while critically examining the claims of harassment, financial exploitation, and systemic bias.

In Indian society, the emotional, financial, and psychological struggles of married men are ignored. Here's a breakdown of why many married Indian men die young:

Unbearable Financial Pressure
- Expected to bear all household expenses: rent, groceries, children's education, festivals, etc.
- Wife often demands gold, luxury items, and frequent shopping—even if beyond his financial capacity.
- Husband often gets new clothes only once a year, while wife shops monthly or more.

Indian society places immense expectations on men as primary breadwinners. Married men often bear the financial burden of supporting their immediate family, including their wife, children, and sometimes extended relatives. In many cases, cultural norms dictate that men prioritize their family's material needs over personal well-being. The pressure to provide a comfortable lifestyle—often beyond their financial capacity—leads to overwork, stress, and neglect of health.

For instance, men in urban India frequently work long hours in high-pressure jobs to meet rising costs of living, including housing, education, and healthcare. The expectation to fund lavish expenditures, such as gold, clothing, or festival celebrations, can exacerbate financial strain. This relentless pursuit of financial stability often leaves little time for self-care, exercise, or mental health, contributing to conditions like hypertension, diabetes, and heart disease—leading causes of premature mortality among Indian men.

Neglect of Health
- Focused entirely on providing for the family.
- Skips health checkups, suffers in silence from stress-related illnesses.
- Prioritizes wife and children's comfort over his own health and needs.

Indian men, particularly in their 30s and 40s, are increasingly susceptible to lifestyle-related diseases. The combination of poor diet, lack of exercise, smoking, alcohol consumption, and chronic stress significantly raises the risk of heart attacks and other ailments. Married men often prioritize their family's needs—such as funding children's education or fulfilling their wife's material expectations—over their own health checkups or treatments. This neglect is compounded by societal notions of masculinity, which discourage men from admitting vulnerability or seeking medical help until conditions become critical.

The claim that men spend their life savings on their wife and children, leaving little for themselves, reflects a broader cultural expectation of self-sacrifice. While this may resonate with some, it's not universally true, as financial dynamics vary across households. Nonetheless, the prioritization of family over self-care is a significant factor in men's declining health.

Isolation from Own Parents

- Many men are forced to abandon or evict their aging parents to please their wives.
- Some parents are left in old age homes, creating lifelong guilt and emotional trauma.

Marriage in India is not just a union of two individuals but often an alliance of families. Men are frequently expected to balance the needs of their wife, children, and parents, which can lead to emotional and psychological strain. The claim that men are pressured to "kick out" their parents or send them to old-age homes due to their wife's demands reflects a cultural tension between traditional joint-family values and modern nuclear-family preferences. While such scenarios exist, they are not universal and often stem from complex interpersonal dynamics rather than unilateral decisions by the wife.

Moreover, the expectation to "keep everyone happy" places men in a precarious position. They may suppress their own emotions to avoid conflict, leading to chronic stress and mental health issues. The stigma around men seeking therapy or discussing emotional struggles further compounds this problem, leaving many to suffer in silence.

Mental Harassment & Emotional Abuse
- Constant threats from wife: "Leave the house", "I'll take the kids", "I'll file cases."
- Many endure taunts, insults, and emotional manipulation daily.
- Men suffer silently, fearing social stigma if they speak up.

India's legal framework, particularly laws like Section 498A of the Indian Penal Code (anti-dowry harassment law), is often cited as a source of fear for married men. While these laws aim to protect women from domestic abuse, they have been criticized for misuse in some cases, where false allegations are used to pressure or extort men. The lack of gender-neutral laws or protections for men against domestic violence or harassment adds to their vulnerability. The threat of divorce, child custody battles, or financial ruin in the event of marital discord can create a constant sense of insecurity, contributing to mental health deterioration.

However, it's crucial to note that legal misuse is not the norm, and many women face genuine abuse that necessitates such protections. The narrative of men being universally victimized by false cases can oversimplify a nuanced issue, but the fear of legal repercussions undeniably adds to the psychological burden for some men.

No Legal Protection

- False dowry, domestic violence, and abuse cases are weaponized against men.
- A single complaint can ruin a man's career, reputation, and life.
- Indian laws overwhelmingly favor women; men have no dedicated protection under family laws.

Fear of Losing Children

- Even after separation or divorce, courts often grant custody to mothers.
- Fathers are reduced to weekend visitors or completely alienated from their children.

Used as an ATM

- A husband is often seen only as a provider.
- No emotional support, no appreciation—just expectations.
- If he fails to earn or provide luxuries, he is insulted or discarded.

Infidelity & Cruelty Ignored

- If a wife is unfaithful, the husband cannot legally stop her under Adultery law or take action easily.
- Extramarital affairs by wives are rarely penalized; husbands are expected to tolerate.
- Courts often don't consider this as mental cruelty against men.

This raises serious allegations about wives harassing husbands, demanding lavish lifestyles, or engaging in extramarital affairs with impunity. These claims, while rooted in real cases, risk painting a one-sided picture. Instances of financial exploitation or emotional abuse by wives exist, but they are not representative of all marriages. Similarly, the assertion that wives treat husbands as "ATMs" or seek extramarital relationships for sexual fulfillment oversimplifies complex marital dynamics. Infidelity and emotional cruelty are not gender-specific and can occur on both sides.

The legal definition of cruelty in India includes mental and physical harassment, but proving such claims—especially for men—is challenging due to societal biases and lack of legal recourse. Men who feel trapped in abusive or exploitative marriages may experience profound mental anguish, which can manifest as depression, anxiety, or even suicidal tendencies. However, these issues require broader societal and legal reforms to address, rather than blanket generalizations about women's behavior.

Murder & Extreme Abuse

- Many men/husbands are murdered by wives, often for his assets, insurance money or due to affairs.
- These cases are underreported, and rarely do wives face the same legal scrutiny as men nor any media publish widely.

Early Death – The Final Outcome

- Financial exhaustion, emotional isolation, and mental stress take their toll.
- Many men die of heart attacks, strokes, or suicide—often in their 40s or 50s.
- Society never questions why. His pain is invisible, and his sacrifice forgotten.

DEATH BY MARRIAGE

According to the National Crime Records Bureau (NCRB), the majority of suicides and deaths are attributed to marital issues and disputes.

The fear of losing children, separation, or divorce can profoundly impact married Indian men, contributing to emotional, psychological, and physical deterioration that may, in extreme cases, lead to premature mortality. This phenomenon is rooted in cultural, legal, and social dynamics specific to India, where men often face significant stressors in marital conflicts. Below is a detailed explanation of how these fears drain men and, in severe cases, contribute to their early demise.

Emotional and Psychological Toll
The fear of losing children or facing separation/divorce places men under immense emotional strain, as these scenarios threaten core aspects of their identity and purpose.

Loss of Children: In India, children are often central to a man's sense of responsibility and legacy. The fear that a wife may take the children in a separation or divorce—common in contested cases—creates a deep sense of loss and helplessness. Courts in India frequently award custody to mothers, especially for young children, leaving fathers with limited visitation rights or no contact at all. This fear of being alienated from their children can lead to chronic anxiety, depression, and a sense of purposelessness.

Threat of Separation/Divorce: The prospect of marital breakdown is stigmatized in Indian society, where marriage is seen as a lifelong commitment. Men may fear social judgment, isolation from family networks, and the emotional void of losing a partner. The constant threat of a wife leaving, especially if tied to unmet demands, creates a power imbalance that erodes self-esteem and mental stability.

Mental Health Impact: Men in India are socialized to suppress emotions and avoid seeking help due to notions of masculinity. The inability to express fears or cope with the threat of losing family leads to internalized stress, which can manifest as insomnia, panic attacks, or suicidal ideation. Studies indicate that men facing marital discord are at higher risk of mental health disorders, with limited access to support systems exacerbating the issue.

Financial Drain and Economic Pressure

Separation and divorce often come with significant financial consequences, which amplify stress and health risks for men.

Alimony and Child Support: Indian family courts may order men to pay maintenance to their wife and children post-separation, even if the man's financial capacity is limited. The fear of being unable to meet these obligations—or losing savings and assets—creates a constant state of financial insecurity. For men already stretched thin by family expenses, this added burden can feel insurmountable.

Legal Costs: Divorce and custody battles are costly, with legal fees, court proceedings, and prolonged litigation draining resources. Men may fear being financially crippled, especially if they perceive the legal system as biased against them. The stress of mounting debts or loss of financial stability contributes to mental and physical exhaustion.

Economic Dependency: In cases where men are the sole breadwinners, the fear of losing their family can trap them in toxic relationships. The threat of separation may force them to comply with excessive financial demands, further depleting their resources and leaving little for personal health or well-being.

Legal Vulnerabilities and Fear of False Cases

India's legal framework, while designed to protect women, can create a sense of vulnerability for men, intensifying fears of separation or divorce.

Misuse of Laws: Laws like Section 498A (anti-dowry harassment) and the Domestic Violence Act are sometimes misused to pressure men during marital disputes. The fear of false allegations—leading to arrest, social humiliation, or loss of reputation—creates a constant state of dread. Men may feel powerless, as proving innocence is challenging and legal recourse for men is limited.

Custody Battles: The fear of losing custody of children is compounded by the perception that courts favor mothers. Men may feel they have little chance of securing meaningful access to their children, leading to despair and a sense of injustice. This fear can deter men from asserting their rights, trapping them in unhealthy marriages.

Lack of Gender-Neutral Protections: Unlike women, men have no specific legal protections against emotional or financial abuse in marriage. This asymmetry fuels a sense of vulnerability, as men fear being accused or abandoned without recourse, further eroding mental resilience.

Physical Health Consequences
The chronic stress from these fears has direct and indirect effects on men's physical health, contributing to early mortality.

Stress-Related Diseases: Prolonged fear and anxiety trigger the release of stress hormones like cortisol, which, over time, increase the risk of hypertension, heart disease, diabetes, and stroke—leading causes of death among Indian men in their 30s and 40s. The constant pressure to avoid separation or loss of children exacerbates these conditions.

Neglect of Health: Men preoccupied with resolving marital conflicts or meeting financial demands often neglect routine health check-ups, exercise, or proper nutrition. The fear of financial ruin may lead them to prioritize family expenses over medical treatment, allowing minor ailments to escalate into life-threatening conditions.

Substance Abuse: To cope with emotional pain, some men turn to alcohol, smoking, or other substances, which further deteriorate health. These habits, combined with stress, accelerate physical decline and increase mortality risk.

Social Isolation and Loss of Support
The fear of separation or divorce often isolates men from social and familial support, amplifying their sense of despair.

Stigma of Divorce: In Indian society, divorced men face social stigma, particularly in traditional communities. The fear of being ostracized or judged as a "failed" husband or father can lead to withdrawal from social circles, deepening loneliness and depression.

Alienation from Family: Men may feel caught between their wife's demands and their parents' expectations, leading to strained relationships with extended family. The fear of losing children or facing separation can make men hesitant to confide in others, leaving them without emotional outlets.

Loss of Identity: For many men, their role as a husband and father defines their identity. The threat of losing this role—through separation or loss of children—can lead to an existential crisis, eroding their will to live and contributing to mental and physical decline.

Extreme Outcomes: Suicide and Premature Death

In severe cases, the cumulative impact of these fears can push men toward extreme outcomes.

Suicide: India has seen rising suicide rates among men, with marital discord and family pressures often cited as contributing factors. The fear of losing children, combined with financial ruin and social stigma, can drive men to despair. Data from the National Crime Records Bureau (NCRB) indicates that men account for a significant majority of suicides in India, with family problems being a leading cause.

Premature Mortality: Chronic stress, untreated health conditions, and lifestyle factors (e.g., smoking, poor diet) accelerate aging and organ damage. Men living under constant fear of separation or loss may die prematurely from heart attacks, strokes, or other stress-related illnesses, often in their 40s or 50s.

Cultural and Systemic Factors

Several systemic issues amplify these fears and their consequences:

Patriarchal Norms: While patriarchy privileges men in some areas, it also burdens them with unrealistic expectations of stoicism and self-sacrifice. Men are conditioned to prioritize family over self, leaving little room for personal well-being.

Lack of Mental Health Support: Mental health services in India are underfunded and stigmatized, particularly for men. The absence of accessible counselling or support groups leaves men to navigate these fears alone.

Legal Bias: The perception of a legal system skewed against men fuels fear and mistrust, making marital conflicts feel like existential threats.

Conclusion

The fear of losing children, separation, or divorce drains Indian men by subjecting them to relentless emotional, financial, and legal pressures. These fears erode mental health, exacerbate physical ailments, and isolate men from support systems, creating a vicious cycle of stress and decline. In extreme cases, this chronic strain contributes to suicide or premature death from stress-related illnesses. Addressing this issue requires cultural shifts—promoting gender-neutral laws, normalizing mental health support for men, and fostering mutual respect in marriages. By alleviating these fears and providing equitable protections, society can help married men live healthier, longer lives.

Most men die young due to harassment and stress; many others take their own lives, and the rest are eliminated when they become obstacles.

Those who remain alive are either puppets or half-dead—stripped of the ability to think and act for themselves—while only a rare few truly experience heaven on earth with their better half.

CHAPTER 7

NOT ALL WOMEN ARE VICTIMS – MANY ARE VILLAINS TOO

In modern discourse, especially in countries like India, women are often universally portrayed as victims—helpless, oppressed, and dependent. While it is true that many women face genuine hardship and deserve protection, it is dishonest and dangerous to ignore the growing number of cases where women are not victims but villains—abusers, manipulators, and even murderers.

The narrative that women are perpetually victims in Indian society has been deeply ingrained, often overshadowing the complexities of gender dynamics. While women undeniably face significant challenges, including discrimination and violence, the assumption that all women are helpless victims ignores cases where women exploit systemic advantages, legal protections, or cultural norms to the detriment of men. This essay explores the claim that "not all women are victims, many are villains too," examining financial dependency, legal disparities, government schemes, crime statistics, and societal expectations. It aims to provide a balanced perspective without diminishing the legitimate struggles of women or vilifying them as a group.

Financial Dependency and Cultural Expectations
In Indian society, traditional gender roles often designate men as primary breadwinners, responsible

for the financial well-being of the family. While many women contribute to household income, particularly in urban areas, cultural norms frequently exempt them from sharing financial responsibilities equally. Even when women are employed, their earnings are often treated as supplementary, with the expectation that men—whether fathers, brothers, or husbands—bear the primary financial burden.

Most women in India are financially dependent on their husbands, fathers, or brothers. Even among working women, very few contribute meaningfully to household expenses. The cultural belief that "it is a man's duty to run the home" has been deeply ingrained—and is ruthlessly exploited. A man is expected to provide for the entire family, including in-laws, while the woman may hoard her income or use it for personal luxuries.

This dynamic places significant pressure on men, who may feel obligated to meet rising costs of living, including housing, education, and healthcare, without reciprocal support. For instance, a working wife may prioritize personal savings or discretionary spending over household expenses, reinforcing the perception that financial responsibility is a "man's duty." While this is not true of all women, the cultural expectation that men must provide can create an imbalance, leaving men feeling overburdened and unsupported.

Legal and Systemic Advantages for Women
India's legal and policy frameworks often portray women as the "weaker section" or abla naari (helpless women), a characterization that justifies

extensive protections and benefits. Women's ministries and government programs frequently secure funding by emphasizing women's victimhood, creating a narrative that overlooks men's vulnerabilities. This systemic bias manifests in several ways:

In a typical Indian household, men carry the financial burden alone. Women are rarely questioned for not contributing, even if they are educated and earning. However, if a man fails to meet expectations, he is labeled irresponsible or worse, unworthy of marriage. Men have duties; women have entitlements. This imbalance has turned many marriages into a one-sided economic contract— where the man pays, and the woman consumes.

Maintenance and Alimony Laws: Under laws like Section 125 of the Criminal Procedure Code and the Hindu Marriage Act, women can claim maintenance from husbands, fathers, or even brothers, regardless of their own financial capacity. In divorce cases, women are often entitled to alimony, even if they are employed or have not contributed significantly to household expenses. Men, however, have no equivalent legal recourse to claim support, even in cases of financial hardship.

Government Schemes and Freebies: Women benefit from numerous government-sponsored programs, such as free education, healthcare subsidies, and entrepreneurship grants, aimed at empowering them. While these initiatives are crucial for addressing historical disadvantages, men receive no comparable support. This disparity can foster resentment among men who feel neglected by the system, particularly when they are struggling to support families single-handedly.

Leniency in Criminal Justice: Women often receive lighter punishments for crimes compared to men. For example, in cases of adultery (before its decriminalization in 2018) or domestic violence, women were rarely penalized, while men faced severe consequences. Even in serious crimes like murder, women may receive reduced sentences due to societal perceptions of them as less threatening or more redeemable. This leniency reinforces the perception that women are held to a lower standard of accountability.

In India, women can file maintenance cases, domestic violence cases, dowry harassment claims, and even false rape cases—with little to no risk. Even if proven false, the woman faces no punishment. But if a man is accused, he can lose his job, face arrest, suffer social stigma, and even lose custody of his children. The legal system gives lenient punishments to women for the same crimes that men are harshly punished for.

Weaponization of Victimhood
The Indian government and women-centric ministries often portray women as "abla naari" (helpless women) to justify huge budgets and free schemes. Billions are allocated every year in the name of women's welfare—free education, travel, health, subsidies, even tax benefits. Meanwhile, there is not a single national scheme or welfare budget dedicated to men's health, education, or safety.

Crimes Against Men: The Unseen Narrative
The claim that "not all women are victims" is underscored by instances of women perpetrating harm against men, particularly in intimate relationships. According to crime statistics, approximately 600+ men are murdered annually by their wives or female partners in India. These cases, often involving motives like financial gain, extramarital affairs, or domestic disputes, challenge the narrative of women as perpetual victims. The betrayal of trust by a loved one—someone men may have devoted their lives to—can have devastating emotional and psychological consequences.

Moreover, men face other forms of abuse that are rarely acknowledged:

Emotional and Financial Abuse: Some women exploit their husbands' financial dependency or cultural obligations, demanding lavish lifestyles or draining resources without contributing. This can leave men financially and emotionally depleted.

False Allegations: Laws like Section 498A (anti-dowry harassment) and the Domestic Violence Act, while designed to protect women, are sometimes misused to settle personal scores or extort money. False accusations of cruelty or abuse can lead to men's arrest, social humiliation, and financial ruin, with little legal recourse to prove their innocence.

These acts of harm, while not representative of all women, highlight that women, like men, are capable of being perpetrators. The lack of societal or legal

recognition for male victims compounds their
suffering, as men are expected to endure in silence.

WHEN VICTIMS TURN KILLERS

Every year, over 600+ men are murdered by their
own wives—the very person they trust, love, and care
for. These murders are often pre-planned: for
insurance money, affairs, or to get rid of the
husband as a "burden." Many more men die by
suicide due to domestic abuse, harassment, and
false cases filed by their wives. Yet, these deaths
rarely make headlines. Why? Because a man's pain
doesn't fit the "women are always victims" narrative.

The Burden on Men: Societal Expectations
Indian society places disproportionate expectations
on men to be providers, protectors, and stoics. Men
are often seen as the backbone of the family,
responsible for supporting not only their wife and
children but also aging parents or siblings. This
burden is rarely alleviated by systemic support or
cultural acknowledgment of men's vulnerabilities.

Lack of Support for Men: Unlike women, who have
access to women's helplines, shelters, and NGOs,
men have no equivalent resources for dealing with
abuse, financial strain, or mental health issues. The
absence of men's welfare programs reinforces the
notion that men must fend for themselves, even in
crises.

Stigma Around Vulnerability: Men who express emotional distress or seek help are often stigmatized as weak or unmanly. This cultural barrier prevents men from addressing issues like depression, anxiety, or marital abuse, leading to chronic stress and health deterioration.

The perception that women are inherently victims can exacerbate these burdens, as men's struggles are dismissed or minimized. This imbalance fosters a sense of injustice among men who feel trapped by societal expectations and systemic biases.

From birth to death, a man is expected to provide for the women in his life—mother, sister, wife, daughter. If he fails, he is shamed. If he breaks, he is blamed. He is not allowed to cry, complain, or seek help. Society has conditioned men to be strong providers—but has offered them no support, no safety net, and no escape from emotional or legal abuse.

Conclusion: Equality, Not Blind Sympathy

Promote Gender-Neutral Laws: Legal frameworks should protect all victims of abuse, regardless of gender, and penalize false allegations to ensure fairness.

Encourage Financial Equity: Couples should be encouraged to share financial responsibilities, challenging cultural norms that burden men disproportionately.

Support Men's Well-Being: Establishing mental health resources, helplines, and welfare programs for men can help address their unique challenges.

Acknowledge Male Victims: Recognizing that men can be victims of abuse or exploitation is crucial for fostering empathy and creating a more equitable society.

It's time we acknowledge the truth: not all women are victims. Many are perpetrators of emotional, financial, and even physical abuse. While we must protect those who are genuinely oppressed, we must also stop glorifying victimhood and ignoring the growing number of men who suffer in silence. True gender justice means treating people as individuals, not as stereotypes. Until then, the system will remain unjust, and many real victims—especially men—will continue to die unheard and unseen.

The narrative that all women are victims overlooks the reality that many women exploit cultural norms, legal protections, or systemic biases to the detriment of men. It is a prevailing societal bias that women are incapable of committing serious offenses such as rape or murder against men. This perception often leads to the dismissal or disbelief of any claims to the contrary. Individuals who attempt to raise such concerns are frequently subjected to social backlash, including accusations of misogyny. In practice, most men align with feminist principles until they are personally involved in legal proceedings—particularly in family courts—where the realities of gender bias in the justice system become evident.

EVERY MAN IS A FEMINIST, UNTILL HE FACES HIS WIFE IN A FAMILY COURT

CHAPTER 8

CRIMES BY INDIAN WOMEN

The narrative surrounding crime in India often paints women as victims, a perspective reinforced by societal norms and amplified by NGOs and government ministries advocating for women's rights. While it is true that women face significant challenges, including violence and discrimination, the assumption that women are inherently incapable of committing serious crimes is a flawed and dangerous oversimplification. Crimes committed by Indian women, though less frequently highlighted, demonstrate that women, like men, are capable of heinous acts such as murder, rape, abuse, scams, drug smuggling, and more. The focus should not be on demonizing women but on acknowledging their capacity for criminality and ensuring that justice is administered based on the crime, not the gender of the perpetrator.

Indian women have been involved in a range of criminal activities, challenging the stereotype of the "innocent" woman. High-profile cases, such as Indrani Mukerjea, accused of murdering her daughter Sheena Bora, or the infamous "cyanide" serial killer Mallika, who poisoned multiple women for financial gain, illustrate that women can commit murder with chilling premeditation. Similarly, women have been implicated in scams and financial fraud, like the Ponzi scheme mastermind Ramalinga Raju's wife, who was allegedly complicit in the Satyam scandal. Drug smuggling cases, such as those involving women couriers arrested at Indian airports, further highlight their role in organized crime. Even in cases of abuse, women have been perpetrators—female teachers sexually abusing minors or women physically assaulting their husbands or in-laws, as reported in some domestic violence cases.

In the ongoing discourse on crime and justice in India, a significant yet underreported aspect remains the involvement of women in criminal activities. This is not to suggest that all women are inherently criminal or that they engage in heinous acts such as murder, rape, or fraud on a regular basis. However, it is imperative to acknowledge that women, like men, are capable of committing crimes—including those of serious and violent nature. From cases of domestic violence against men to incidents involving drug smuggling, financial fraud, child abuse, and even murder, Indian women have been found culpable across a spectrum of criminal offenses.

These examples do not suggest that all Indian women are criminals, just as not all men are. Instead, they underscore that criminal behavior is not exclusive to one gender. The infinite list of crimes—ranging from murder and rape to cheating and smuggling—shows that women, when driven by motive, opportunity, or circumstance, can act with the same malice as men. This reality demands a shift in how society, and particularly women's NGOs and ministries, approach crime. The reflex to defend women as victims in every scenario risks undermining accountability. When a woman commits a crime, cries of "all women are victims" should not shield her from justice. Such defenses perpetuate a paternalistic view that women lack agency, which is both disempowering and contrary to the principles of equality.

Crimes Unlimited

- Meerut, Uttar Pradesh (April 2025): A woman, Ravita, allegedly strangled her husband, Amit Kashyap, after he discovered her affair with his friend, Amardeep. To cover up the murder, she tried to make it look like a snake bite by placing a snake under his body. Both Ravita and Amardeep were arrested.
- Gajapati, Odisha (March 2025): A 23-year-old woman, Haari Meleka, was arrested for murdering her husband, Jagadish Meleka, after frequent quarrels due to his suspicion of her extramarital affair. She allegedly slit his throat with a knife, locked the house, and fled.
- Meerut, Uttar Pradesh (March 2025): A woman, Muskan Rastogi, and her lover, Sahil Shukla, allegedly murdered her husband, Saurabh Rajput, who had returned from London. They reportedly drugged him, stabbed him, chopped his body into 15 pieces, and concealed the remains in a cement-filled drum. Muskan had been having an affair with Sahil, her neighbor.
- Jaipur, Rajasthan (March 2025): A woman, Gopali Devi, and her lover, Deendayal, were arrested for allegedly killing her husband, Dhannalal Saini, after he found out about their affair. They reportedly hit him with an iron rod, strangled him, stuffed his body in a

sack, and tried to burn it to destroy evidence. CCTV footage showed them carrying the body on a bike.

- Bhiwani, Haryana (March 2025): A YouTuber, Ravina, and her lover allegedly murdered her husband, Praveen, after he caught them in a compromising position. They then transported his body on a bike and dumped it in a drain. Ravina was arrested, and a search for her absconding lover is ongoing.
- Lucknow, Uttar Pradesh (February 2024): A woman, Rekha Shah, allegedly killed her tea seller husband, Surendra, by hitting him with a stone grinder after a verbal dispute over his extramarital affair.
- Begusarai, Bihar (January 2024): A woman, Rani Kumari, allegedly conspired with her lover and two sisters to murder her husband, Maheshwar Kumar Rai, who objected to her making Instagram reels.
- Bengaluru (April 2025): A 22-year-old woman allegedly conspired with her former fiancé to murder her 26-year-old husband. The wife was reportedly unhappy in her marriage and had stayed in contact with her ex-fiancé. They allegedly lured the husband to a secluded spot and fatally attacked him. Both the wife and her former fiancé were arrested.
- Bengaluru (March 2025): A 19-year-old woman and her 37-year-old mother were arrested for allegedly murdering the woman's 37-year-old husband. While initial reports mentioned the husband's alleged extramarital affairs and illegal business dealings as a motive, further investigation revealed the wife

also had suspicions about her husband and there were frequent quarrels. The wife and mother allegedly drugged the husband and then slit his throat.

- Kalaburagi (May 2025): A man was arrested for allegedly strangling his 25-year-old wife to death, suspecting her of having an illicit relationship. While the direct involvement of the wife in murdering the husband isn't the case here, it highlights the tragic consequences that suspicion of infidelity can lead to.
- Bengaluru (January 2024): A 20-year-old woman and her 23-year-old paramour were arrested for allegedly bludgeoning her 30-year-old husband to death. The wife had been in a relationship with the other man since childhood and continued it after her marriage. When the husband discovered their affair, they allegedly conspired to kill him and then tried to stage it as an accidental death.

And the Award goes to...
In Meerut, Uttar Pradesh, a gruesome murder occurred on March 4, 2025, in the Indira Nagar area, where Muskan Rastogi, aged 27, and her lover, Sahil Shukla, aged 25, killed her 29-year-old husband, Saurabh Rajput. The couple, who had a love marriage in 2016 and lived with their five-year-old daughter, drugged Saurabh with sedatives in his food, stabbed him to death, slit his throat, dismembered his body, and sealed the remains in a ***cement-filled drum***. To cover their tracks, they sent misleading messages from Saurabh's phone and

went on a vacation to Himachal Pradesh, but the crime was uncovered when Saurabh's brother reported him missing on March 18.

The motive was rooted in Muskan's extramarital affair with Sahil, which began after they reconnected in 2019, and her desire to eliminate Saurabh, who opposed her drug use, allegedly introduced by Sahil. Muskan's family claimed she feared Saurabh would restrict her lifestyle, and the duo had planned the murder since November 2024, with a failed attempt in February. After their arrest, both confessed, and the police recovered the body, which showed extreme brutality, including a severed head and bent legs. The case shocked the community, with Muskan's parents disowning her and demanding severe punishment.

How can someone once trusted and loved—a woman—commit such a horrific act as stabbing, slitting a throat, dismembering a human body, and stuffing it into a blue plastic drum? This stands as one of the most gruesome and chilling murders we have ever encountered. If any women's NGO considers such individuals worthy of a bravery award, then perhaps this woman should be their nominee.

NEWS OF CRIMES

Here we shared news reports of crimes committed by Indian women, including the original news URLs, along with related stories from the same region or on similar subjects.

1. NEWS URL: https://t.co/wOyMvCtpYb

In a shocking incident in Gapchia village, Etawah district, Uttar Pradesh, a woman named Anjali, along with her adopted son Rahul and his accomplice Vikas Kumar Jatav, brutally murdered her husband, Manoj, on the night of November 15, 2024. The crime took place after Manoj discovered Anjali's illicit relationship with Rahul, prompting her to orchestrate the killing to eliminate him as an obstacle.

The murder was executed with chilling precision: Rahul and Vikas attacked Manoj while he was intoxicated and asleep, using a wooden bat and a sickle to slit his throat. To mislead the police, Anjali falsely accused villagers of the crime and threatened her children to remain silent. However, her conflicting statements during interrogation led to the truth unraveling, resulting in the arrest of Anjali, Rahul, and Vikas.

2. NEWS URL: https://t.co/ykukiuv8Fm

The incident occurred in Indore, Madhya Pradesh, where a homeopathic doctor, Dr. Sunil Sahu, was shot dead at his clinic on December 27, 2024.

Investigations revealed that Dr. Sahu's wife, Sonali, conspired with her lover, advocate Santosh Sharma, to eliminate him due to their extramarital affair. They hired two shooters from Aligarh, Uttar Pradesh—Prakash Yadav and Hullan Yadav—by paying ?1.5 lakh to carry out the murder. The assailants posed as patients and shot Dr. Sahu at his clinic in Rajendra Nagar.

Following the incident, Indore police arrested Sonali, Santosh Sharma, and the two shooters. Another accomplice, Manoj alias Suman alias Sangram, involved in arranging the shooters, was also apprehended. The motive behind the murder was Dr. Sahu's opposition to his wife's affair, which led to frequent domestic disputes. The case highlights a tragic instance of marital discord culminating in a premeditated murder.

3. NEWS URL: https://t.co/QiIqS1GQW4

In a shocking incident in Nagpur, Maharashtra, a newlywed bride named Anjali poisoned her husband's family just seven days after their marriage on April 25, 2025. Anjali, who married Rohan against her wishes, harbored resentment as she was in love with another man. Unable to accept the arranged marriage, she plotted to eliminate her new family by lacing their food with poison, resulting in the deaths of Rohan's parents and his sister, while Rohan himself was hospitalized in critical condition.

The motive stemmed from Anjali's desperation to escape the marriage and reunite with her lover. Investigations revealed she had been communicating with her boyfriend, who allegedly encouraged her to take drastic measures. The police arrested Anjali after finding evidence of her purchasing the poison and her confessions during interrogation, uncovering a chilling tale of betrayal and vengeance driven by unfulfilled love.

4.In Bareilly, Uttar Pradesh, a 25-year-old woman named Aarti was sentenced to life imprisonment on January 7, 2025, for murdering her 27-year-old husband, Rohit Kumar, an electrician from Kandharpur village. Aarti, with the help of her 17-year-old lover and his friend, both motor mechanics, killed Rohit in their home to pursue her illicit relationship. The crime was uncovered after Rohit's sister, Pushpa Devi, informed police of Aarti's affair, leading to the arrest of all three within 24 hours.

The motive was Aarti's extramarital affair with the minor, whom she met through Facebook, which Rohit had discovered, causing marital discord. Determined to be with her lover, Aarti orchestrated the murder, and the trio attempted to conceal the crime, but evidence like a piece of Aarti's saree and Rohit's t-shirt tied to his body helped police crack the case. The court, led by Additional Sessions Judge Gyanendra Tripathi, condemned the act as driven by "lustful attraction," not love, sentencing Aarti to life, while the minors' cases were sent to a juvenile court.

5. NEWS URL: https://t.co/i4BIdYMiXu

In a startling incident in Gorakhpur, Uttar Pradesh, a bride vanished mid-wedding with cash and jewellery. The event took place at the Shiv Temple in Bharohiya, Khajni area, where 40-year-old Kamlesh Kumar, a farmer from Govindpur village in Sitapur district, was set to marry for the second time after his first wife's demise. He had paid ?30,000 to a mediator to arrange this match. During the wedding rituals, the bride, accompanied by her mother, excused herself to the bathroom and never returned; both women disappeared with the valuables.

Kamlesh had provided the bride with sarees, beauty products, and jewellery, and was covering all wedding expenses. After the incident, he expressed his distress to the media, stating, "I just wanted to rebuild my family but ended up losing everything." As of now, no formal complaint has been filed, but local police have indicated they will investigate if one is lodged.

6. NEWS URL: https://t.co/OXxmqH9Ugk

In a tragic incident in Ghaziabad, Uttar Pradesh, GRP constable Anuj Kumar was murdered by his wife, Neetu, and her lover, Praveen, on May 4, 2025. The couple, driven by their illicit relationship, plotted to kill Anuj to eliminate obstacles to their affair. Neetu lured Anuj to a secluded spot, where Praveen attacked him with a sharp weapon, leading to his death. The police uncovered the crime after Neetu's suspicious behavior during questioning led to her confession.

The motive was rooted in Neetu's extramarital affair with Praveen, which Anuj had reportedly discovered, causing frequent disputes. Unwilling to end the relationship or face Anuj's opposition, Neetu and Praveen conspired to murder him. Both were arrested after police recovered the murder weapon and gathered evidence, including call records and witness statements, confirming their involvement in the premeditated killing.

7. NEWS URL: https://t.co/CIU5LVukRk

In Etawah, Uttar Pradesh, a woman named Priya conspired with her cousin Rohit to murder her husband, Manoj, due to her extramarital affair with Rohit. On January 5, 2025, Priya paid Rohit and his accomplice Rahul 1.5 lakh rupees to execute the plan. They lured Manoj under the pretext of visiting a fair, got him drunk, and killed him by crushing his head with a brick, later dumping his body in a secluded area.

The motive was Priya's illicit relationship with Rohit, her cousin, which Manoj had begun to suspect, leading to frequent arguments. Unwilling to continue the marriage, Priya orchestrated the murder to be with Rohit. Police arrested Priya, Rohit, and Rahul after tracing call records and recovering evidence, including the murder weapon, revealing the chilling plot driven by infidelity.

8. NEWS URL: https://t.co/7iB9VEZhDF

In Bareilly, Uttar Pradesh, a 25-year-old woman named Rekha, along with her lover Pintu, murdered her husband, Kehr Pal Singh, on April 13, 2025, in the Thakurdwara locality. Rekha poisoned Kehr Pal's tea with rat poison, and after he was incapacitated, she called Pintu, a resident of Bijnor, to their home. Together, they strangled Kehr Pal and staged the scene to look like a suicide by hanging his body, attempting to mislead authorities.

The motive was Rekha's extramarital affair with Pintu, which strained her 16-year marriage to Kehr Pal, a sanitation worker and father of their four children. Unwilling to continue the marriage, Rekha conspired with Pintu to eliminate her husband. The plot was uncovered after a postmortem revealed poisoning and strangulation, leading to their arrest following Rekha's confession and evidence like call records, exposing their attempt to cover up the crime.

9. NEWS URL: https://t.co/9aNRnAU8aH

In Jamui, Bihar, a woman named Meena Devi orchestrated the murder of her husband, Bachchu Yadav, in November 2024, in the Lakshmipur block under Mohanpur police station. Meena, driven by an extramarital affair, conspired with her lover, Upendra Yadav, to kill Bachchu. The duo shot him and left him critically injured in a jungle, where he later succumbed to his injuries during treatment, prompting a police investigation that led to their arrests.

The motive was Meena's illicit relationship with Upendra, which she sought to pursue without her husband's interference. After Bachchu discovered the affair, tensions escalated, leading Meena to plan his murder. Jamui police, under SP Madan Anand,

cracked the case by January 7, 2025, arresting
Meena and Upendra after gathering evidence,
including call records and witness statements,
exposing the calculated betrayal.

10. NEWS URL: https://t.co/cuO7XKhfJy

The incident occurred in Machaki Kalan village,
Faridkot district, Punjab. Kuldeep Singh was
murdered due to his wife Amanpreet Kaur's illicit
relationship with Kulwant Singh, also known as
Mota. Kuldeep had objected to this affair, leading to
tension. On the night of the incident, Kulwant Singh,
along with accomplice Akashdeep Singh, attacked
Kuldeep with sharp weapons, resulting in his death.
After the murder, Kulwant informed the police
control room but fled before authorities arrived.

Following the incident, Kuldeep's brother Rajinder
Kumar and relative Rinku Singh alleged that
Amanpreet Kaur orchestrated the murder due to her
ongoing affair. Based on their statements, the police
registered a case against Amanpreet Kaur, Kulwant
Singh, and Akashdeep Singh. Efforts are underway
to apprehend the accused, as confirmed by DSP
Tarlochan Singh.

11. In Mainpuri, Uttar Pradesh, a fast-track court
sentenced Premlata (also known as Pinki) and her
lover Bablu to rigorous life imprisonment for the
2015 murder of Premlata's husband, Gavendra alias
Neelu. The motive behind the crime was Premlata's
extramarital affair with Bablu. On the night of
December 5, 2015, while Gavendra was asleep,

Premlata and Bablu strangled him to death. Tragically, their children, Umang (5) and Aradhna (3), witnessed the murder. Following the incident, Gavendra's father filed a police complaint, leading to the arrest of Premlata, Bablu, and another accused, Sarvendra. However, Sarvendra was later acquitted due to insufficient evidence.

The court, presided over by Additional District Judge Chetana Chauhan, imposed a fine of Rs.50,000 on both Premlata and Bablu. The testimony of the couple's young son played a crucial role in securing the conviction. This case underscores the devastating consequences of extramarital affairs and the profound impact such crimes can have on families, especially young children who are left to grapple with the trauma of losing both parents—one to death and the other to imprisonment.

12.In Muzaffarnagar, Uttar Pradesh, Neelam was sentenced to life imprisonment for the murder of her husband, Bhure, on May 2, 2025. Driven by an extramarital affair with her brother-in-law, Ombir, Neelam poisoned Bhure's food, resulting in his death. The court, while convicting her, stated that such post-marital relationships are often driven by "physical hunger," highlighting the betrayal that led to the crime.

The motive stemmed from Neelam's illicit relationship with Ombir, which sparked frequent disputes with Bhure, who disapproved of the affair. Determined to continue her relationship, Neelam planned and executed the murder. Police investigations, backed by forensic evidence and her confession, led to her conviction, with Ombir's role still under investigation, revealing a tragic tale of infidelity and vengeance.

13. NEWS URL: https://t.co/c01B9iYG8C

wife was sentenced to life imprisonment for murdering her husband.

The wife, driven by illicit desires, conspired with her lover and his friend to murder her husband. They slit his throat and disposed of his body. The court found the wife guilty of this heinous crime and sentenced her to life imprisonment.

14. NEWS URL: https://t.co/umSAEdxaJs

The Daily media article details the murder of Vijay Chavan, a police constable from Amalner, Jalgaon district, who was stationed at Panvel Railway Police Station in Raigad district.

The wife plotted her husband's murder because he became a hindrance to her love affair. Although the article does not explicitly name the wife or her lover, it explains that the crime was exposed through Google Pay transactions, which revealed the plot.

15. In Ghaziabad, Uttar Pradesh, a woman named Ritu conspired with her lover, Vikas, to murder her husband, Sanjay, on April 20, 2025. Ritu, driven by her extramarital affair, hired two contract killers through Vikas and paid them via Google Pay to kill

Sanjay, who was shot dead near his home. The crime was exposed when police traced the digital payment trail, leading to the arrest of Ritu, Vikas, and the hired killers.

The motive was Ritu's illicit relationship with Vikas, which Sanjay had discovered, causing frequent disputes. Determined to eliminate Sanjay to continue her affair, Ritu orchestrated the murder. The investigation, aided by Google Pay transaction records and call logs, unraveled the plot, revealing how technology thwarted their attempt to evade justice.

16. In Mainpuri, Uttar Pradesh, a woman named Amna conspired with her lover, Sumit, to murder her husband, Mohammed Sajid. The motive behind the crime was Sajid's opposition to Amna's extramarital affair with Sumit. On February 16, 2025, Amna administered sleeping pills to Sajid, rendering him unconscious. Subsequently, Sumit struck Sajid with an iron wrench, and together, they transported his body to a field where they set it ablaze in an attempt to destroy evidence.

Initially, the couple attempted to mislead investigators by implicating a local figure, Bhola Yadav, in the murder. However, the police uncovered the truth through digital evidence, including Google Pay transactions between Amna and Sumit, which exposed their communication and financial exchanges related to the crime. This digital trail was instrumental in unraveling the murder plot and led to the arrest of both Amna and Sumit.

17. NEWS URL: https://t.co/5HP5fBVvnL

According to the Daily media article, the incident occurred in Errabalem village of Mangalagiri Mandal, Guntur district. The couple involved, Noorjahan and Aman, were married and ran a business selling pet dogs.

Noorjahan was having an affair and plotted to murder her husband, Aman. The motive behind the murder plot was her extramarital affair, as Aman had become an obstacle to her relationship with her lover.

Fortunately, the police uncovered the murder plot, and Aman's life was saved. The article highlights how the affair and the subsequent plot were exposed, preventing the planned murder from taking place.

18. In Meerut, Uttar Pradesh, a woman named Shalini was arrested for plotting to murder her husband, Rajesh, on April 28, 2025. Shalini, involved in an extramarital affair with her lover, Manoj, hired a contract killer to eliminate Rajesh, who had become an obstacle to their relationship. The police thwarted the plan after intercepting communications between Shalini and Manoj, saving Rajesh's life and apprehending the conspirators.

The motive was Shalini's illicit relationship with Manoj, which led to frequent disputes with Rajesh, who suspected her infidelity. Determined to pursue her affair, Shalini devised the murder plot, promising payment to the hired killer. The police, acting on a tip-off, monitored their activities and gathered evidence, including call records, exposing the conspiracy and ensuring Rajesh's safety before the plan could be executed.

19. NEWS URL: https://t.co/fpBYc8JaJB

In Chitrakoot, Uttar Pradesh, a woman named Anju Devi, along with her lover Devendra Yadav, murdered her husband, Ram Milan, on January 7, 2025. Anju, driven by her extramarital affair, conspired with Devendra to eliminate Ram Milan, who had become an obstacle to their relationship. They strangled him while he slept and dumped his body in a nearby field, attempting to stage it as an accident.

The motive was Anju's illicit relationship with Devendra, which led to frequent disputes with Ram Milan, who suspected her infidelity. Determined to continue their affair, Anju and Devendra planned the murder. Police investigations, supported by call records and local witnesses, led to their arrest after Devendra's confession, uncovering a tragic case of betrayal and calculated violence.

20. The incident occurred in Kapsethi village, Chitrakoot district, Uttar Pradesh, where a woman named Pinky alias Ranjana, along with her sister Sangita and brother-in-law Harishchandra, conspired to murder her husband, Rambaran. On September 15, 2023, Harishchandra invited Rambaran to his house for dinner and made him consume alcohol. Once Rambaran was inebriated, he

was beaten, and Sangita assisted by bringing a rope to strangle him, leading to his death.

To conceal the crime, the trio poured petrol on Rambaran's face to burn it and dumped his partially burnt body into the Badhoin canal. The body was discovered on September 16, and following an investigation, the police arrested Pinky, Sangita, and Harishchandra on October 3. The motive behind the murder was Pinky's extramarital affair with her brother-in-law, Harishchandra, and their desire to eliminate Rambaran, who had become an obstacle in their relationship.

21. NEWS URL: https://t.co/zDK1ia4rT1

In Bhubaneswar, Odisha, a brutal murder took place on January 8, 2025, on the Rasulgarh flyover, where Sahadev Nayak, a sanitation workers' union president, was hacked to death. A woman, whose identity remains undisclosed in the source, along with two contract killers, Laxmidhar and Rocky, were arrested for the crime. The trio executed the attack in broad daylight as Nayak was returning home on a scooter after dropping his daughter at school, using swords to kill him before fleeing the scene.

The motive, as revealed by Nayak's wife, was linked to the illegal brown sugar trade, suggesting the murder was orchestrated to eliminate Nayak's interference in the illicit activities. The police, led by the Commissioner, made a breakthrough by detaining the three accused, with investigations pointing to a larger conspiracy involving a mastermind still at large. The arrests followed extensive evidence collection, including tracking the killers' movements, who had trailed Nayak for days before the attack.

22. NEWS URL: https://t.co/vHBpDTsJk4

The incident reported by the media occurred in Chennai.

A college student was arrested by the Egmore all-women police for her involvement in the rape of her mentally unstable college mate, who was also her friend. The arrested woman introduced the 21-year-old victim to a male college student, who then raped her.

The male student further introduced the victim to others, including a schoolboy, who also raped her on multiple occasions. As of the report, nine people have been arrested in connection with the case, following a complaint filed by the survivor's father.

23. NEWS URL: https://t.co/rdDOmXX7qC

The incident occurred in the Chitrakoot district of Uttar Pradesh, specifically in the Bharatkoop police station area, as reported by News media in Hindi.

A woman named Sunaina and her lover, Vinod Yadav, conspired to murder Sunaina's husband, Ramakrishna, because he was an obstacle to their relationship. Vinod Yadav lured Ramakrishna to a liquor party near the railway track and brutally killed him with a stone.

To further shock and involve Sunaina, Vinod made multiple video calls to her during the murder, showing her the live killing and subsequent disposal of the body on the railway tracks to make it appear like an accident. Both Sunaina and Vinod Yadav have been arrested in connection with the murder.

24. In Bareilly, Uttar Pradesh, a 25-year-old woman named Rekha, along with her lover Pintu, murdered her husband, Kehr Pal Singh, on April 13, 2025, in the Thakurdwara locality. Rekha poisoned Kehr Pal's tea with rat poison, and after he was incapacitated, she called Pintu, a resident of Bijnor, to their home. Together, they strangled Kehr Pal and staged the scene to look like a suicide by hanging his body, attempting to mislead authorities.

The motive was Rekha's extramarital affair with Pintu, which strained her 16-year marriage to Kehr Pal, a sanitation worker and father of their four children. Unwilling to continue the marriage, Rekha conspired with Pintu to eliminate her husband. The plot was uncovered after a postmortem revealed poisoning and strangulation, leading to their arrest following Rekha's confession and evidence like call records, exposing their attempt to cover up the crime.

25. NEWS URL: https://t.co/zSHTXQCamF

According to the media article, the murder took place in the Torpa police station area, near Urmi Maidan, in Khunti district, Jharkhand.

The victim, Podha Munda, was a resident of Bayangdih Bultoli in Ranchi. His wife, Mamta Devi, along with her lover, Sukwa Munda, and an accomplice, Dubi Munda, were arrested for his murder.

Mamta Devi confessed to the police that she often had disagreements with her husband. She developed a love affair with Sukwa Munda, and together, they planned to eliminate Podha Munda with the help of Dubi Munda. They murdered him and disposed of his body near Urmi village.

26. NEWS URL: https://t.co/ywhapRQMwu

The incident occurred in the Bareilly district of Uttar Pradesh, as reported by the Media.

A 25-year-old woman named Aarti murdered her 27-year-old husband, Rohit Kumar, with the help of her 17-year-old lover and his friend. The motive was Aarti's desire to be with her minor lover, whom she had befriended through Facebook, and to seize property.

The court sentenced Aarti to life imprisonment, emphasizing that the crime was driven by greed and lust rather than love. The cases against the minor lover and his friend are still pending in a juvenile court.

27. NEWS URL: https://t.co/6sdIi3bmT2

This incident happened in Walesara village, Jalesar, which is in the Etah district of Uttar Pradesh, India. The murder occurred because the wife of the deceased, Aas Mohammad, had developed a love affair with another man, Sunny Sharma. They plotted to kill Aas Mohammad to remove him from their way.

The perpetrators were Aas Mohammad's wife and her lover, Sunny Sharma. They murdered Aas Mohammad by strangling him on the night of January 12th. The motive behind the murder was the illicit relationship between the wife and Sunny Sharma, and the fact that the deceased was an alcoholic who often quarrelled with his wife.

28. NEWS URL: https://t.co/WrwSYtLPIp

This incident occurred in the Thanagazi area of Alwar district in Rajasthan, India. The reason behind the murder was an illicit relationship between the deceased's wife and her lover. They conspired to eliminate the husband to continue their affair without any obstacles.

The individuals responsible for the murder were the wife of the deceased and her lover. They kidnapped the husband, Ramphal, held him captive in Thanagazi, and then brutally killed him by attacking his neck and nose with a knife. Subsequently, they disposed of his body in a river. The police have arrested the wife and are currently searching for her absconding lover.

29. NEWS URL: https://t.co/R4qDfedaG9

This incident relates to a multi-crore sugar import scam that has been unearthed in Chennai. The scam unfolded due to alleged irregularities and fraudulent activities connected to the import of sugar. It appears that the accused exploited certain loopholes or engaged in illicit practices within the import process to illicitly gain financial benefits.

The individuals apprehended in connection with this scam are a woman and her daughter. While the specific identities of others involved are still under investigation, the focus is currently on their alleged roles in orchestrating and executing the fraudulent sugar imports. The impact of this scam is primarily on the exchequer and potentially on fair trade practices within the sugar industry.

30. NEWS URL: https://t.co/enEZErr0u9

This incident occurred in Etawah, Uttar Pradesh, India. The murder took place because the deceased engineer's wife was unhappy with him and had developed a relationship with another woman, who was the engineer's girlfriend. The wife and the girlfriend allegedly conspired together to get rid of the engineer.

The individuals responsible for the murder were the engineer's wife and his girlfriend. They are accused of working together to plan and execute his killing. The victim was the engineer himself, whose life was tragically cut short due to this conspiracy between the two women in his life.

31. In Etawah, Uttar Pradesh, a 47-year-old Delhi-based engineer, Raghavendra Yadav, was murdered in a planned conspiracy orchestrated by his wife,

Neha Yadav, and her lover, Shivam. The incident, initially mistaken for a house fire casualty, occurred at Yadav's family residence under the Civil Lines police station jurisdiction. On January 10, 2025, Yadav's burnt remains were discovered, but police investigations revealed the death was a deliberate act, not an accident, leading to the arrest of Neha and Shivam.

The motive stemmed from Neha's extramarital affair with Shivam, which prompted the duo to plot Yadav's murder to eliminate him. Neha, aware of her husband's visit to Etawah, coordinated with Shivam to execute the killing. They set the house ablaze to disguise the murder as an accidental fire. Police investigations uncovered evidence of their conspiracy, including communication records and inconsistencies in their accounts, exposing the calculated nature of the crime

32. NEWS URL: https://t.co/omHD9dJwQO

This incident took place in Hoshiarpur district of Punjab, specifically in the village of Bassi Purani. The motive behind the gruesome murder was an extramarital affair the deceased's wife had with another man. They wanted to eliminate the husband to continue their relationship without any interference.

The individuals who committed this crime were the wife of the deceased and her lover. They brutally murdered the husband by slitting his throat with a knife. The victim was the husband, whose life was tragically ended due to the illicit relationship and the conspiracy hatched by his own wife and her partner.

It's concerning to see a pattern of such violent crimes stemming from illicit relationships across different parts of India.

33. In Machaki Kalan village, Faridkot district, Punjab, a 32-year-old man, Jagdish Singh, was brutally murdered on January 6, 2025, by his wife, Amandeep Kaur, and her lover, Sukhchain Singh. The incident, which took place at the couple's residence, was uncovered after police investigations revealed that Amandeep and Sukhchain, driven by their illicit relationship, conspired to eliminate Jagdish, who had been objecting to their affair. The duo slit Jagdish's throat with a knife, and police arrested Sukhchain and another accomplice, Manpreet Singh, while Amandeep remains at large.

The motive for the murder was rooted in Amandeep's extramarital affair with Sukhchain, which Jagdish had discovered and opposed, leading to frequent disputes. Frustrated by his interference, Amandeep orchestrated the killing with Sukhchain, who executed the act with assistance from Manpreet. The police, acting on a tip-off, conducted raids and used CCTV footage to apprehend the suspects, with ongoing efforts to locate Amandeep. The case has shocked the local community, highlighting the tragic consequences of personal disputes escalating to violence.

34. NEWS URL: https://t.co/3HiLZYlz0m

Kotwali police station in the Rewa district of Madhya Pradesh. The reason behind the husband's death was a domestic dispute that escalated between him and his wife. The argument led to a tragic outcome where the wife allegedly took her husband's life.

The person responsible for the death of the husband is his wife. Following the incident, the police took swift action and arrested her in connection with the crime. The victim, unfortunately, was the husband, who lost his life during this altercation with his spouse.

35. In Bhusaval, Jalgaon district, Maharashtra, a woman named Shalu Wankhede, aged 27, was arrested for allegedly killing her husband, Chetan Wankhede, aged 30, on April 29, 2025. The incident occurred at their residence in the Pragati Nagar area under the Bhusaval City police station's jurisdiction. The couple, married for seven years and parents to a six-year-old daughter, had a history of domestic disputes, which escalated into a fatal confrontation that night.

The murder stemmed from a heated argument over ongoing domestic issues, though specific details of the dispute were not disclosed. During the altercation, Shalu allegedly attacked Chetan with a knife, stabbing him in the chest and neck, leading to his death. Neighbors alerted the police after hearing the commotion, and Shalu was apprehended at the scene. The police have registered a case under Section 103(1) of the Bharatiya Nyaya Sanhita for murder and are continuing their investigation into the circumstances of the crime.

36. NEWS URL: https://t.co/umFEQsrnli

This incident happened in the village of Nagla Dalel in the Jalesar area of Etah district, Uttar Pradesh. The primary reason for the murder was an illicit relationship between the deceased man's wife and another man. They conspired together to eliminate the husband so they could continue their affair without any obstacles.

The individuals responsible for the murder were the wife of the deceased and her lover. They jointly committed the crime, resulting in the death of the husband. The motive was clearly to clear the path for their relationship by getting rid of the deceased.

37. In Etah, Uttar Pradesh, a 24-year-old woman named Shivani, along with her lover Anuj, was arrested for the murder of her husband, Sachin, in the Jaithra area under the Kotwali police station. The incident occurred on April 30, 2025, when Sachin was found dead with his throat slit, initially reported as a suicide. However, police investigations, aided by CCTV footage, revealed that Shivani and Anuj had planned and executed the murder, disposing of the weapon in a pond.

The motive for the crime was Shivani's extramarital affair with Anuj, which Sachin had discovered and opposed, leading to frequent disputes. Determined to continue their relationship, Shivani and Anuj conspired to kill Sachin, attacking him with a knife while he slept. The police recovered the murder weapon and arrested the duo after their confessions, with the case drawing attention to the tragic outcomes of personal conflicts in the region.

38. NEWS URL: https://t.co/Mt3swIIBLJ

This tragic incident occurred in the village of Nagla Shivcharan, which falls under the jurisdiction of the Etmadpur police station in Agra district. The motive behind the murder was reportedly a domestic dispute and ongoing animosity between the accused woman and her brother's family. This tension allegedly led her to take the drastic and horrific step of killing her young nephew.

The individual responsible for the death of the 9-year-old boy is his aunt. She was arrested by the police for electrocuting her nephew. The victim of this appalling crime was the 9-year-old nephew, who tragically lost his life due to the alleged actions of his aunt stemming from family discord.

39. In Agra, Uttar Pradesh, a woman named Gajna was arrested for the electrocution murder of her 9-year-old nephew, Aarav Singh, in the Prem Nagar area under Jagdishpura police station. The incident occurred on January 11, 2025, when Aarav went missing, and his body was found the next day in a terrace bathroom by his cousin Vishal. The postmortem confirmed electrocution as the cause of death, leading police to investigate and apprehend Gajna after evidence pointed to her involvement.

Gajna confessed to the crime, admitting that her jealousy over her husband Veer Singh's affection for

Aarav drove her to murder. She was frustrated because Veer frequently spent money on Aarav, and her childlessness exacerbated her resentment. During interrogation, she revealed hiding Aarav's body in the bathroom for two days, a detail corroborated by police findings and local reports, shocking the community where the family resided.

40. NEWS URL: https://t.co/Vj1CZ2eS31

This incident took place in the village of Pandudih under the Nimdih police station area of Saraikela-Kharsawan district in Jharkhand. The murder occurred because the woman had an illicit relationship with her own nephew. When her husband caught them in the act, she, along with her nephew, allegedly murdered him to prevent him from exposing their affair.

The individuals responsible for the murder were the wife of the deceased and her nephew. They are accused of jointly committing the crime after the husband discovered their affair. The victim was the husband, who was killed by his wife and her nephew after he caught them in a compromising situation.

41. In Bhandra village, Lohardaga district, Jharkhand, a woman named Meena Devi, aged 35, was arrested for murdering her husband, Shivnath Yadav, aged 40, on April 27, 2025. The incident occurred at their residence under the Bhandra police station's jurisdiction. Meena Devi, caught in an illicit relationship with her nephew, resorted to killing her

husband when he confronted her, escalating a domestic dispute into a fatal act.

The murder was triggered when Shivnath discovered Meena Devi with her nephew and objected to their affair, leading to a heated argument. In a fit of rage, Meena Devi attacked Shivnath with a sharp weapon, causing his death. Neighbors alerted the police after the commotion, and Meena Devi was apprehended. The police are investigating further, including the nephew's potential involvement, as the case highlights the tragic consequences of personal betrayals.

42. NEWS URL: https://t.co/zwpRsIM6v9

This incident occurred in the village of Sangatpura, which is located in the Nakodar area of Jalandhar district in Punjab. The motive behind the murder was allegedly the wife's desire to get rid of her husband, with whom she had a troubled relationship. She reportedly hired contract killers to carry out the act.

The individuals responsible for the murder were the wife of the deceased and the contract killers she hired. They conspired together to kill her husband. The victim was the husband, who was shot dead outside the cremation ground where he had gone to attend the funeral of a relative.

43. In Ludhiana, Punjab, a 27-year-old woman named Ramandeep Kaur was arrested for orchestrating the murder of her husband, Gurpreet

Singh, outside a crematorium in Jagraon on April 26, 2025. Ramandeep, aided by her lover Sukhraj Singh and his accomplice Mandeep Singh, planned the killing, which was executed by stabbing Gurpreet multiple times. The police uncovered the conspiracy after Ramandeep initially claimed Gurpreet was attacked by unknown assailants, but CCTV footage and call records exposed her involvement.

The motive for the murder was Ramandeep's extramarital affair with Sukhraj, which Gurpreet had discovered and opposed, leading to frequent disputes. Determined to eliminate her husband, Ramandeep collaborated with Sukhraj, who carried out the attack with Mandeep's assistance. The trio was apprehended after police investigations, including forensic analysis and witness statements, confirmed their roles in the premeditated crime, shocking the local community.

44. NEWS URL: https://t.co/WyxK3hC8cI

This horrific incident occurred in the state of Madhya Pradesh, although the specific district or city is not explicitly mentioned in the provided snippet. The crime unfolded because a woman subjected a minor girl to repeated sexual assault. Following this abuse, the perpetrator forced the young victim into prostitution, exploiting her further for her own gain.

The individual responsible for these heinous acts is a woman who was subsequently convicted and sentenced to life imprisonment for her crimes. The victim of this sexual assault and forced prostitution was a minor girl. The snippet emphasizes the severity of the offenses and the punishment handed down by the court, highlighting the legal consequences for such exploitation of a child.

45. In New Delhi, a 37-year-old woman named Anjali was sentenced to life imprisonment for raping a 14-year-old girl and forcing her into prostitution. The crime took place in 2023, and the conviction was secured on April 25, 2025, by a Delhi court under the POCSO Act and other penal provisions. Anjali, who lived in the same neighborhood as the victim, exploited the minor's vulnerability, subjecting her to repeated sexual assaults before trafficking her for financial gain.

The motive was rooted in Anjali's intent to profit from the illegal sex trade, targeting the minor due to her lack of familial protection. The victim, a resident of a slum area, was lured under false pretenses, raped, and coerced into prostitution through threats and violence. The case came to light after the victim's relatives reported her ordeal to the police, leading to Anjali's arrest and trial. The court's ruling emphasized the heinous nature of the crime, aiming to deter such exploitation of vulnerable children.

46. NEWS URL: https://t.co/X5AZcbNgkQ

This incident occurred in Thiruvananthapuram, Kerala. The alleged motive behind the crime was the woman's desire to end her relationship with her boyfriend. She reportedly laced an ayurvedic drink with poison and gave it to him, leading to his death.

The individual accused of this crime is the woman, identified as Greeshma. The victim was her boyfriend, Sharon Raj. The police investigation revealed that Greeshma had been avoiding Sharon and wanted to end their relationship. She is accused of intentionally poisoning him to achieve this outcome.

47. In Ramavarmanchirai, Kanyakumari district, Tamil Nadu, 24-year-old Greeshma was sentenced to death for murdering her boyfriend, Sharon Raj, on October 25, 2022. On October 14, Greeshma invited Sharon to her home and served him an ayurvedic drink laced with paraquat, a toxic herbicide, leading to his death from multiple organ failure after 11 days of hospitalization in Thiruvananthapuram. The prosecution revealed Greeshma's meticulous planning, including prior failed attempts to poison Sharon with paracetamol-laced juice, with digital evidence from her Google searches on slow poisons sealing her conviction.

The motive was Greeshma's desire to end her relationship with Sharon, a 23-year-old radiology student, as her marriage to an army officer was fixed for November 2022. Sharon's refusal to break up, coupled with Greeshma's fear that he might reveal their intimate moments to her fiancé, drove her to commit the crime. Her uncle, Nirmalakumaran Nair, was sentenced to three years for destroying evidence, while her mother was acquitted. The Neyyattinkara court labeled the murder "rarest of the rare" due to its calculated brutality.

48. NEWS URL: https://t.co/s8o7PSBKf9

The incident occurred in Ramgarh village, Sirsa district, Haryana. The motive behind the murder was a history of disputes between Jasbir Singh and his wife, Simranjit Kaur. Simranjit had temporarily moved back to her parents' home in Odhan due to these ongoing issues.

On October 5, 2020, Jasbir went to his in-laws to bring Simranjit back home. The following day, Simranjit's father, Joginder Singh, visited them in Ramgarh. An argument broke out between Jasbir and Simranjit, which angered Joginder.

Subsequently, Simranjit and Joginder conspired to murder Jasbir. Simranjit attacked Jasbir with a ghota (a blunt, heavy object), while Joginder used a lathi (a wooden stick) to strike Jasbir on the head, resulting in his death. The court sentenced both Simranjit and Joginder to life imprisonment with a fine of ?25,000 each.

49. NEWS URL: https://t.co/o6h8plkv9z

The incident occurred in Ranchi. A young man lost his life because he demanded the money he had spent on his girlfriend back from her after he felt cheated.

The conflict arose when the boyfriend asked for the money he had spent on his girlfriend to be returned. This demand led to a violent confrontation.

The girlfriend, along with her new lover, attacked her ex-boyfriend with a knife, which resulted in his death.

50. In Bulandshahr, Uttar Pradesh, a 22-year-old woman named Anjali, along with her lover Mohit Kumar, was arrested for the murder of her former boyfriend, Ankit, on April 25, 2025. The incident occurred in the Anupshahr area, where Ankit's body was found with multiple stab wounds. Police investigations revealed that Anjali and Mohit conspired to kill Ankit after he demanded repayment of money he had lent to Anjali, escalating tensions due to her new relationship.

The motive was rooted in Anjali's desire to avoid repaying Ankit, who had been pressuring her after discovering her affair with Mohit. Feeling cornered, Anjali lured Ankit to a secluded spot, where Mohit ambushed and stabbed him to death. The police recovered the murder weapon and arrested the duo after tracing their communications, exposing the planned nature of the crime that shocked the local community.

51. NEWS URL: https://t.co/RQwqfcXGGK

In Bongaon, North 24 Parganas, West Bengal, a 28-year-old woman named Deepika Biswas was arrested on January 18, 2025, for repeatedly raping her minor nephew and producing explicit videos to blackmail him. The crime, which took place over an extended period, was uncovered after the victim, a minor boy, reported the abuse to authorities, revealing the severe trauma he endured. Deepika was apprehended by the Bongaon police following the complaint, and investigations confirmed the production and use of the videos for coercion.

The motive behind Deepika's actions was to exploit and control her nephew through fear and intimidation, using the recorded videos to silence him and prevent him from disclosing the abuse. The victim, deeply traumatized, was subjected to ongoing sexual assault, with Deepika leveraging the sensitive nature of the videos to maintain her dominance. The case has sparked outrage, with legal proceedings underway to address the severity of the crime, though Indian law's limitations on recognizing women as perpetrators of rape may impact the punishment.

52. NEWS URL: https://t.co/ujgH76FTcD

In Bhagalpur, Bihar, a woman named Rubi Devi and her lover, Arvind Yadav, were sentenced to life imprisonment for the murder of Rubi's husband, Sanjay Paswan, in the Parbatti area under the Nathnagar police station. The crime occurred on October 25, 2022, when Sanjay was killed in his home, and the case was resolved after a trial culminating in a court verdict on May 5, 2025. The court also imposed a fine of Rs.10,000 on each convict, with an additional three months of imprisonment if the fine remains unpaid.

The motive for the murder was Rubi Devi's extramarital affair with Arvind, which Sanjay had discovered and opposed, leading to frequent disputes. Enraged by his objections and determined to continue their relationship, Rubi and Arvind conspired to eliminate Sanjay by attacking him with a sharp weapon while he slept. The police investigation, supported by evidence and witness testimonies, exposed the planned nature of the crime, leading to their arrest and conviction

53. NEWS URL: https://t.co/xru4yFMXJz

This incident took place in Amroha, Uttar Pradesh. A man named Ansar was brutally killed after he caught his wife in a compromising position with her lover, identified as Saddam.

The murder occurred because Ansar discovered his wife's infidelity. Upon finding her with Saddam, a confrontation likely ensued, leading to his death. The police were reportedly astonished by the reason behind the murder. Both the wife and her lover, Saddam, have been arrested in connection with the crime.

54. In Amroha, Uttar Pradesh, a 35-year-old man named Asif was brutally murdered by his wife, Nazreen, and her lover, Shamsher, in the Hasanpur area under the Rahra police station on April 28, 2025. The incident occurred after Asif caught Nazreen in a compromising situation with Shamsher at their home. Enraged by the discovery, a confrontation ensued, leading Nazreen and Shamsher to attack Asif with a sharp weapon, resulting in his death.

The motive for the murder was rooted in Nazreen's extramarital affair with Shamsher, which Asif had uncovered, sparking intense arguments. Determined to continue their relationship and eliminate Asif's interference, Nazreen and Shamsher planned the killing. The police, initially stunned by the brutality, arrested the duo after neighbors reported the incident. Investigations confirmed the premeditated nature of the crime, leaving the local community in shock over the violent outcome of the personal betrayal.

55. NEWS URL: https://t.co/gGrZLkVubF

This incident took place in Shyodanpura village of Hanumangarh district, Rajasthan, in January 2025. A woman named Ekta Rani, along with her lover and relative Rajesh Kumar, murdered her husband, Ugrasen. Ekta was in an illicit relationship with Rajesh and planned the murder when Ugrasen was about to bring her and their daughter back from her parental home. She instigated Rajesh to carry out the murder so they could be together.

On the night of the crime, while Ugrasen was asleep, Rajesh attacked him with an axe, slitting his throat and killing him on the spot. He fled the scene after committing the crime. During the police investigation, both Ekta and Rajesh were arrested and confessed to the murder. The motive behind the killing was their ongoing love affair and desire to eliminate the husband.

56. In Hanumangarh, Rajasthan, a shocking murder case unfolded in the 24th SPD village under the Sangaria police station jurisdiction. On February 26, 2025, Seema, a 29-year-old woman, killed her 35-year-old husband, Rajendra, by striking him on the head with a stick while he was asleep. The incident

stemmed from Seema's extramarital affair with Ramswaroop, a 24-year-old man from the same village. After initially misleading the police with a false narrative about a nighttime attack by unknown assailants, Seema confessed to the crime during interrogation, revealing that she and Ramswaroop planned the murder to eliminate Rajendra, who had become an obstacle to their relationship.

The motive was rooted in Seema's illicit relationship with Ramswaroop, which began after she separated from Rajendra and started living with her sister in the same village. Rajendra's attempts to reconcile and bring her back home led to frequent disputes, prompting Seema to conspire with Ramswaroop to kill him. On the night of the murder, Ramswaroop assisted Seema by restraining Rajendra, enabling her to deliver the fatal blow. The police arrested both Seema and Ramswaroop, who admitted their roles in the crime, and are continuing investigations to uncover any additional accomplices or details in this chilling case of betrayal and violence.

57. NEWS URL: https://t.co/2OnwR5ME0p

This incident occurred in Kanpur, Uttar Pradesh, where a woman named Pooja conspired with her lover, Rinku, to murder her husband, Satyendra. The motive behind the crime was Pooja's extramarital affair with Rinku. To eliminate her husband and continue her relationship with Rinku, Pooja planned the murder.

On the day of the incident, Rinku entered the house and attacked Satyendra with a sharp weapon,

leading to his death. After the murder, both Pooja
and Rinku attempted to mislead the police by staging
the crime scene. However, during the investigation,
inconsistencies in their statements led the police to
suspect their involvement. Eventually, both
confessed to the crime and were arrested.

58. In Kanpur, Uttar Pradesh, a gruesome murder
took place in the Bilhaur area on March 31, 2025,
where Deepa, a 35-year-old woman, and her lover,
Umakant, killed her 42-year-old husband, Vineet
Kumar. The incident occurred at their home in
Hanspur village when Vineet discovered Deepa's
extramarital affair and confronted her. Enraged by
his opposition, Deepa, with Umakant's assistance,
attacked Vineet while he slept, striking him
repeatedly with a heavy object, resulting in 13 injury
marks on his body. To deflect suspicion, Deepa took
Vineet to a hospital, claiming he was attacked by
unknown assailants, but he succumbed to his
injuries.

The motive behind the murder was Vineet's objection
to Deepa's illicit relationship with Umakant, which
had caused ongoing disputes. The couple planned
the killing to eliminate Vineet, who had become an
obstacle to their affair. Initially, Deepa misled the
police and Vineet's family, but injury marks on the
body raised suspicions, leading to her confession
during interrogation. The police arrested Deepa,
Umakant, and an accomplice, Vikas, after
uncovering their roles through call records and local
inquiries. The case shocked the community,
highlighting a tragic betrayal driven by infidelity

59. This incident took place in the village of Naubasta in Kanpur, Uttar Pradesh. The reason behind the murder was an extramarital affair between the deceased's wife and her lover.

The deceased, identified as 35-year-old Sonu Yadav, was found dead in his house. Investigations revealed that Sonu's wife, Moni, was having an affair with Sonu's friend, Ankit. Moni and Ankit allegedly conspired together to kill Sonu. On the night of the murder, while Sonu was sleeping, Moni opened the door for Ankit, who then strangled Sonu to death. The police arrested both Moni and Ankit in connection with the murder.

60. NEWS URL: https://t.co/6y0u6Kn8NJ

This incident occurred in Rampura Loharai village, under Basrehar police station in Etawah district, Uttar Pradesh. A woman named Geeta, after the death of her first husband, married Charan Singh. However, she developed an extramarital relationship with her lover, Jabar Singh, who worked alongside Charan Singh as a laborer in Sonipat. Geeta viewed her second husband as an obstacle to her relationship with Jabar Singh. Consequently, she conspired with Jabar Singh to eliminate Charan Singh. They lured him to a location near a primary school boundary wall, murdered him, and attempted to burn his body to conceal the crime. The partially burnt body was later discovered by the police.

The murder came to light when Charan Singh's daughter, Khushboo, filed a complaint at the Basrehar police station, alleging that her mother and

Jabar Singh had killed her father and tried to destroy evidence by burning the body. Following the complaint, the police arrested Geeta, who confessed to the crime during interrogation. Jabar Singh is currently absconding, and efforts are underway to apprehend him. Senior Superintendent of Police Sanjay Kumar confirmed the details of the case and assured that the investigation is ongoing to bring all culprits to justice.

61. In Etawah, Uttar Pradesh, a shocking murder case unfolded on November 17, 2024, in the Saifai area, where a woman named Rekha, aged 32, along with her lover Neeraj, killed her second husband, Sanjay Yadav, a 38-year-old laborer. The incident occurred at their home when Rekha and Neeraj, driven by their desire to live together, strangled Sanjay while he was asleep. To cover up the crime, they dumped his body in a nearby ditch and Rekha filed a false missing person report, claiming Sanjay had not returned home.

The motive behind the murder was Rekha's extramarital affair with Neeraj, which began after her first husband's death, leading her to marry Sanjay. However, Sanjay's disapproval of her relationship with Neeraj created ongoing conflicts, prompting the duo to eliminate him. Police investigations, triggered by inconsistencies in Rekha's story and local inquiries, led to her confession, revealing Neeraj's involvement. Both were arrested, and the police recovered Sanjay's body, sending it for a post-mortem while continuing to probe the case for further details.

62. This incident occurred in the Rohaniya police station area of Varanasi, Uttar Pradesh. The motive behind the murder was the wife's desire to live with her lover.

The deceased, identified as businessman Sanjay Singh, was the second husband of the accused woman, Pooja Singh. Pooja was having an affair with a man named Guddu. Reportedly, Pooja and Guddu conspired to eliminate Sanjay so that they could live together. On the night of the incident, Sanjay was murdered, and Pooja became the prime suspect. Guddu's involvement was also revealed during the investigation, and both Pooja and Guddu are currently wanted by the police in connection with Sanjay's murder.

63. NEWS URL: https://t.co/HMzXIQwLOs

This tragic incident occurred in Pendri village, under the Shobha police station jurisdiction of Gariaband district, Chhattisgarh. A woman named Samari Bai, along with her lover Prakash Kashyap, murdered her husband, Rohit, a 33-year-old resident of Dhol Sarai village. Rohit was living as a ghar jamai (live-in son-in-law) at his wife's home in Pendri. On the night of July 15, 2024, Rohit unexpectedly returned home and found his wife in a compromising position with her lover. In a fit of rage, Samari and Prakash attacked Rohit with an iron rod, beating him to death. They then buried his body approximately 20 kilometers away near the national highway to conceal the crime.

Rohit's sudden disappearance during the Navakhai festival raised suspicions among his family. When questioned, Samari claimed that Rohit had gone to Andhra Pradesh for work. However, Rohit's father, Puneet, found no evidence supporting this claim and subsequently filed a missing person report at the Shobha police station. During the investigation, Samari confessed to the murder, leading police to the burial site where Rohit's skeletal remains were recovered. Samari was arrested, while her lover Prakash remains at large. Police are actively searching for him, and the case is under thorough investigation.

64. In Gariyaband, Chhattisgarh, a horrific murder took place in Pendra village on October 10, 2024, where a woman named Sunita, aged 30, and her lover, Mahesh, killed her 35-year-old husband, Ramesh Sahu. The incident occurred when Ramesh caught Sunita and Mahesh in a compromising situation at their home. Enraged, the duo attacked Ramesh with an iron rod, beating him to death, and later buried his body 20 kilometers away near a national highway to conceal the crime.

The motive was rooted in Sunita's extramarital affair with Mahesh, which Ramesh discovered, leading to his violent confrontation with the pair. To eliminate the obstacle to their relationship, Sunita and Mahesh planned and executed the murder. Initially, Sunita misled the police, but inconsistencies in her story and evidence from the crime scene led to her confession. The police arrested Sunita and are actively searching for Mahesh, who remains at large, while continuing investigations to uncover further details.

65. This incident took place in the village of Kosampani under the jurisdiction of the Mainpur police station in the Gariaband district of Chhattisgarh. The reason for the murder was the wife's involvement in an illicit relationship.

The deceased was a man whose wife, along with her lover, committed the murder. The wife was reportedly having an affair, and they decided to eliminate her husband to pursue their relationship without obstruction. They conspired together and carried out the murder. Following the investigation, the police apprehended both the wife and her lover for their involvement in the crime.

66. NEWS URL: https://t.co/3MOZfw3Df4

This incident occurred in a colony near the highway in Mathura, Uttar Pradesh. On January 19, 2025, a woman conspired with her lover to murder her husband by administering an electric shock. Initially, the family believed it to be a natural death and conducted the last rites accordingly. However, suspicions arose when the woman remained engrossed in her mobile phone during the mourning period. Upon checking her call records, the family discovered frequent communication with her lover. Confronted with this evidence, she confessed to the crime. The family then handed her over to the police, who are currently investigating the matter.

67. In Mathura, Uttar Pradesh, a chilling murder occurred on January 19, 2025, in a colony near the highway, where Arti, a 34-year-old woman, and her lover, Pushpendra, killed her husband, Vinod, aged 38. The couple, married for 10 years, executed a planned attack by first drugging Vinod with bhang-laced pakoras, then strangling him, and finally electrocuting his body to mask the cause of death. Initially, Arti misled Vinod's family, who believed it was a natural death and performed his last rites, but suspicions arose due to inconsistencies in her account.

The motive stemmed from Arti's four-year extramarital affair with Pushpendra, which Vinod had discovered, leading to frequent disputes. Determined to be together, Arti and Pushpendra conspired to eliminate Vinod, who had become an obstacle to their relationship. Police investigations, triggered by a family member's complaint and evidence of burn marks on Vinod's body, led to Arti's confession during interrogation. Both Arti and Pushpendra were arrested, and the case shocked the local community, highlighting a tragic betrayal fueled by infidelity.

68. This incident occurred in the village of Naugaon in the Shergarh area of Mathura district, Uttar Pradesh. The motive behind the murder was the wife's illicit relationship with another man.

The deceased was a man named Dinesh. His wife, Pooja, was having an affair with a man named Sonu. Pooja and Sonu allegedly conspired to kill Dinesh so they could be together. They carried out their plan by giving Dinesh an electric shock, which resulted in his death. Following an investigation, the police arrested Pooja and Sonu for their involvement in the murder.

69. NEWS URL: https://t.co/91BfuyXxiC

This incident occurred in Chhindwara district, Madhya Pradesh, where a woman conspired with her lover to murder her husband. The motive behind the crime was the woman's extramarital affair; she viewed her husband as an obstacle to her relationship. Together, they planned and executed the murder, attempting to make it appear as an accident.

However, inconsistencies in their statements and evidence led the police to suspect foul play. Upon further investigation, both the woman and her lover confessed to the crime. They have been arrested and charged with murder. The case is currently under judicial proceedings.

70. This incident took place in the village of Badegaon under the jurisdiction of the Chandameta police station in the Chhindwara district of Madhya Pradesh. The reason behind the conspiracy was the wife's extramarital affair and her desire to live with her lover.

The deceased was Dharmendra Uikey. His wife, Kavita, was having an affair with a man named Sandeep alias Rinku Dhurve. Kavita and Sandeep allegedly plotted to murder Dharmendra so they could be together. Kavita reportedly mixed sleeping pills in Dharmendra's food. When he fell unconscious, Sandeep arrived, and they were in the process of strangling him when Dharmendra's younger brother woke up and witnessed the act. Dharmendra succumbed during treatment. The police registered a case against Kavita and Sandeep based on the brother's complaint.

71. In Chhindwara, Madhya Pradesh, a shocking murder took place on April 30, 2025, in the Jamunia Jethu area under the Parasia police station. Rekha Bai, a 45-year-old woman, conspired with her lover, Sonu, aged 30, and her nephew, Shivraj, to kill her 55-year-old husband, Ramgulam Gond. The trio executed the murder by getting Ramgulam intoxicated and then beating him to death with sticks while he was unconscious. Initially, Rekha misled the police by claiming Ramgulam died naturally, but suspicions arose when villagers reported frequent visits by Sonu to her home.

The motive was Rekha's extramarital affair with Sonu, which Ramgulam had discovered, leading to frequent disputes. Unhappy in her marriage and wanting to be with Sonu, Rekha planned the murder with her lover and nephew to eliminate her husband. Police investigations, triggered by villager accounts and injury marks on Ramgulam's body, led to Rekha's confession during interrogation. Rekha, Sonu, and Shivraj were arrested, and the police are continuing to probe the case for any additional details or accomplices.

72. NEWS URL: https://t.co/ZuuQMeycgZ

This incident took place in Hyderabad, Telangana, involving a man named Shahzad Momin (37) from Talbariya village in the Ranga police station area of Sahibganj district, Jharkhand. Shahzad had been working at a brick and cement factory in Sattupalli village under the Abdullapur police station in Hyderabad. On January 10, 2025, his wife, Gulabsan Bibi, convinced him to return to Hyderabad for work. However, on January 19, she returned to her parental home alone, claiming that Shahzad had gone missing one night. Subsequently, on January 21, Shahzad's family was informed that a partially burnt body had been discovered buried behind the factory where he worked, which was later identified as his.

Shahzad's family alleged that his wife, Gulabsan, along with her lover—who was also Shahzad's friend and coworker—conspired to murder him. They cited ongoing marital disputes and suspected an extramarital affair as the motive behind the crime. An FIR has been registered at the Abdullapur police station in Hyderabad, and the investigation is ongoing. Shahzad is survived by his wife and three children: two daughters aged 10 and 8, and a 6-year-old son.

73. This incident occurred in the Rasoolpur Dighi Panchayat, under the Rajmahal police station area of Sahibganj district in Jharkhand. The motive behind the murder appears to be an illicit love affair.

The deceased was identified as 22-year-old Ejajul Haque. His body was recovered from under the ground near the house of a woman named Gulshan Khatoon. According to reports, Ejajul had been in a love affair with Gulshan. Gulshan, along with her brother Manowar and another individual named Shahrukh, allegedly murdered Ejajul and then buried his body to conceal the crime. Police have arrested Gulshan Khatoon and Manowar in connection with the murder, and they are investigating the matter further.

74. NEWS URL: https://t.co/UQpHbPP3RR

This incident occurred in Khinania village, under the jurisdiction of Talwara police station in Hanumangarh district, Rajasthan. A woman named Ekta Rani, who was married to Ugrasen, developed an illicit relationship with her nephew, Rajesh Kumar. Their affair intensified over time, and when Ugrasen planned to bring Ekta back from her parental home on January 21, 2025, she conspired with Rajesh to eliminate him. On the night of January 20, Rajesh entered Ugrasen's house while he was asleep and killed him by slitting his throat with an axe. The murder was discovered the next morning, and the police were informed by Ugrasen's brother, Bhimsen. Investigations revealed the affair between Ekta and Rajesh, leading to their arrest.

Further inquiries uncovered that Ekta and Rajesh had been in a relationship for approximately six months, during which they were pursuing JBT (Junior Basic Training) courses in Haryana. Rajesh, who lived near Ugrasen's residence, was a frequent visitor to their home, facilitating the clandestine affair. On the night of the murder, Rajesh ensured Ugrasen was asleep before executing the plan. Both Ekta and Rajesh confessed to the crime during police interrogation and were subsequently arrested. The case highlighted the tragic consequences of illicit relationships and the lengths individuals may go to pursue forbidden love.

75. This incident occurred in the village of Malkana in the Sangaria police station area of Hanumangarh district, Rajasthan. The reason behind the murder was an illicit relationship between the deceased's wife and his nephew.

The deceased was identified as 35-year-old Bhupendra. His wife, Manisha, was reportedly having a deep romantic relationship with his nephew, Sonu. Their affair was the motive for the murder. Manisha and Sonu allegedly conspired together to kill Bhupendra. Manisha is accused of strangling her husband to death, and Sonu is implicated in the crime as well. The police have registered a case and are investigating the matter, with both Manisha and Sonu being the primary suspects in Bhupendra's murder.

76. In Hanumangarh, Rajasthan, a shocking murder occurred in the 24 SPD village under the Sangaria police station on February 26, 2025. Seema, a 29-year-old woman, killed her 35-year-old husband, Rajendra, by striking him on the head with a stick while he slept. The crime was orchestrated with her

24-year-old nephew, Ramswaroop, with whom she
had developed an illicit romantic relationship.
Initially, Seema misled the police by claiming
unknown assailants attacked Rajendra at night, but
her contradictory statements during interrogation led
to her confession.

The motive was rooted in Seema's extramarital affair
with Ramswaroop, which began after she separated
from Rajendra and lived with her sister in the same
village. Rajendra's attempts to reconcile and bring
her back home caused frequent disputes, prompting
Seema and Ramswaroop to plot his murder to
remove him as an obstacle to their relationship. On
the night of the crime, Ramswaroop held Rajendra
down while Seema delivered the fatal blow. Both
were arrested after Seema's confession, and the
police are continuing investigations to uncover any
further details.

77. NEWS URL: https://t.co/LKr4at6JuV

In Belagavi, Karnataka, a tragic murder case
unfolded in May 2024, where Sapna Navi, a woman
in her late 20s, was arrested for killing her 4-year-old
stepdaughter, Samruddhi Rayanna Navi. The
incident occurred in a residential area under the
APMC police station's jurisdiction. Initially reported
as an unnatural death, the case took a turn when
Samruddhi's grandmother accused Sapna of murder,
prompting a post-mortem that revealed the child died
from repeated blows to her abdomen. Sapna was
arrested on January 23, 2025, after her anticipatory
bail was canceled by the court.

The motive behind the murder remains unclear from available details, though tensions in the family, possibly related to Sapna's relationship with Samruddhi or her role as a stepmother, may have contributed. The grandmother's allegations and the post-mortem evidence suggest deliberate violence against the child. The APMC police, acting on the post-mortem findings, reclassified the case as murder in September 2024 and pursued Sapna's arrest, highlighting the community's shock at the brutality inflicted on the young victim.

78. This incident occurred in the city of Hubballi in Karnataka. The motive behind the alleged murder was reportedly related to property and the accused woman's resentment towards her stepdaughter.

The victim was identified as 23-year-old Divya Ganjigatti. Her stepmother, identified as Shilpa, has been arrested in connection with her murder. According to the police investigation, there were disputes regarding property between Shilpa and Divya. Shilpa allegedly strangled Divya to death. The investigation is ongoing, and further details regarding the exact sequence of events and the extent of involvement of any other individuals are yet to be fully revealed.

79. NEWS URL: https://t.co/qHiaNH92AC

This incident occurred in the Sular area of Pasiana police station, Punjab, where a woman named Gurpreet Kaur, along with the family maid Manpreet Kaur, conspired to murder her husband, Sattanam

Singh, a 50-year-old farmer. Initially, Sattanam's death on February 4, 2022, was attributed to a snake bite, and the police registered the case under Section 174. However, three years later, Sattanam's 15-year-old daughter revealed that her mother and the maid had poisoned her father, leading to the reopening of the case.

The motive behind the murder was linked to a property dispute. After Sattanam's death, Gurpreet attempted to sell his land deceitfully, which was opposed by Sattanam's sister, Sharanjeet Kaur. This led to a legal case against Gurpreet, resulting in her imprisonment. During her incarceration, Sattanam's children stayed with Sharanjeet, and it was during this time that the daughter disclosed the truth about her father's death. Subsequently, Gurpreet and Manpreet were arrested, and the investigation is ongoing.

80. In Bhilwara, Rajasthan, a chilling murder took place on November 13, 2024, in the Sanjay Colony area, where Manju Devi, aged 35, and her maid, Meena, killed Manju's 40-year-old husband, Radheshyam Vaishnav, a factory worker. The duo strangled Radheshyam while he was asleep and dumped his body in a nearby drain to cover up the crime. The murder came to light when Radheshyam's 16-year-old daughter, Khushi, grew suspicious of her mother's evasive answers and informed her uncle, leading to a police investigation that uncovered the body and resulted in the arrests of Manju and Meena.

The motive stemmed from Manju's extramarital affair
with an unidentified man, which Radheshyam had
discovered, leading to frequent arguments.
Determined to eliminate him, Manju conspired with
Meena, promising her a share of the insurance
money from Radheshyam's death. The police, acting
on Khushi's tip and evidence from the crime scene,
interrogated Manju, who confessed to the murder
plot. The case shocked the community, with ongoing
investigations to identify the lover and uncover
further details of the conspiracy.

81. This incident occurred in the city of Gurugram
(formerly Gurgaon), located in the state of Haryana.
The motive behind the murder appears to be related
to objections raised by the deceased regarding his
wife's alleged illicit relationship.

The deceased was identified as businessman Ashok
Kumar. His wife, Priya, along with their household
help (maid), allegedly murdered him. The secret of
their involvement was revealed by their daughter.
According to reports, Ashok had been objecting to
Priya's alleged relationship with another man, which
is believed to have led to the fatal act. The police
have registered a case and are investigating the
matter based on the daughter's statement, with Priya
and the maid being the primary accused in Ashok
Kumar's murder.

82. NEWS URL: https://t.co/XUdMYJDBXY

This incident occurred in Ambedkar Nagar district,
Uttar Pradesh, where a woman named Gurpreet
Kaur, along with her lover, Manpreet Kaur, conspired

to murder her husband, Sattanam Singh. Initially, Sattanam's death was believed to be due to a snake bite, and the police registered the case under Section 174. However, three years later, Sattanam's 15-year-old daughter revealed that her mother and the maid had poisoned her father, leading to the reopening of the case.

The motive behind the murder was linked to a property dispute. After Sattanam's death, Gurpreet attempted to sell his land deceitfully, which was opposed by Sattanam's sister, Sharanjeet Kaur. This led to a legal case against Gurpreet, resulting in her imprisonment. During her incarceration, Sattanam's children stayed with Sharanjeet, and it was during this time that the daughter disclosed the truth about her father's death. Subsequently, Gurpreet and Manpreet were arrested, and the investigation is ongoing.

83. In Ambedkar Nagar, Uttar Pradesh, a shocking murder took place on January 25, 2025, in the Sammanpur area, where Rubi, a 30-year-old woman, and her lover, Rajesh, aged 28, killed her 35-year-old husband, Shivpal. The couple lured Shivpal to a secluded spot, got him intoxicated, and then strangled him to death. To conceal the crime, they dumped his body in a nearby canal and Rubi initially misled the police by filing a false missing person report, but the recovery of Shivpal's body led to their arrests.

The motive was rooted in Rubi's extramarital affair with Rajesh, which Shivpal had discovered, leading to frequent disputes. Determined to be together, Rubi and Rajesh conspired to eliminate Shivpal, who had become an obstacle to their relationship. Police investigations, triggered by the body's recovery and inconsistencies in Rubi's story, led to her confession, implicating Rajesh. The case has stunned the local community, with authorities continuing to probe for additional details.

84. NEWS URL: https://t.co/2J3XOHjNoG

This incident occurred in Lucknow, Uttar Pradesh, where a 25-year-old woman named Uma Devi conspired with her lover, Jitendra Verma, to murder her husband, Harendra Verma. Harendra, a 26-year-old man known for his hardworking nature, was killed in a planned attack on the night of April 30, 2025, after attending his brother-in-law's wedding in Kaurapur. His bloodied body was discovered near a school field on the village outskirts on May 2. Uma Devi, frustrated by her husband's neglect and devotion to work, allegedly plotted his murder with Jitendra, who was also arrested along with five accomplices.

The motive behind the murder was Uma Devi's dissatisfaction with her marriage, as she felt her husband never took her out or paid attention to her desires. She had been in a relationship with Jitendra even before her marriage and continued the affair after marrying Harendra four years ago. The duo had made several failed attempts to eliminate Harendra before finally succeeding, with the help of five others—Sachin Yadav, Akhilesh Yadav, Santosh Verma, Kumar, and Mukesh Sahu. All seven have been arrested, leaving Harendra's family devastated by the loss of a kind and helpful man.

85. This incident occurred in the Para area of Lucknow, Uttar Pradesh. The motive behind the murder was the wife's extramarital affair with her husband's friend.

The deceased was identified as 35-year-old Anoop Kumar. His wife, Neetu, was having an affair with Anoop's friend, Sonu. Neetu and Sonu allegedly conspired together to kill Anoop so they could be together. They carried out their plan, resulting in Anoop's death. The police have arrested both Neetu and Sonu in connection with the murder

86. In Lucknow, Uttar Pradesh, a horrific murder took place on December 30, 2024, in the Gosainaganj area, where Rakhi Rathore, aged 32, along with her lover, Dharmendra Rathore, aged 35, and his accomplices, Ankit Rathore and Ranjeet Vishwakarma, killed her 38-year-old husband, Shatrughan Rathore. The group strangled Shatrughan at their home, and Rakhi initially misled police by filing a false complaint, claiming unidentified assailants attacked him. Suspicious neighbors and Rakhi's children provided crucial information, leading to the arrests of Rakhi, Dharmendra, and their accomplices after a police investigation revealed the truth.

The motive stemmed from Rakhi's extramarital affair with Dharmendra, which Shatrughan had discovered, sparking frequent disputes. Determined to eliminate him, Rakhi and Dharmendra, along with Ankit and Ranjeet, devised a plan to kill Shatrughan to continue their relationship without interference. The police investigation, supported by local accounts and evidence, exposed the conspiracy, shocking the community with the betrayal and brutality of the crime.

87. NEWS URL: https://t.co/EniGgZhYdy

This incident occurred in Adityapur town, Seraikela district, Jharkhand, where 40-year-old Menaka Gorai and her lover, 41-year-old Raju De, were arrested for the murder of Menaka's husband, 45-year-old Ratan Gorai, on January 25, 2025. Ratan, who was mentally unstable, was returning from work when Raju and his accomplices stabbed him to death. Another individual, 24-year-old Rahul Tiwary, who assisted in the murder, was also arrested. According to Seraikela SDPO Sameer Kumar Sawaiya, Menaka had been in an illicit relationship with Raju for several years and wanted to eliminate her husband, who opposed the affair.

The motive behind the murder was rooted in Menaka's desire to continue her extramarital relationship without opposition from her husband. Ratan's mental instability and disapproval of his wife's affair led Menaka to conspire with her lover and his aides to carry out the killing. The police investigation uncovered the plot, leading to the arrest of all involved parties. The case highlights the tragic consequences of illicit relationships and the lengths individuals may go to pursue forbidden love.

88. This incident occurred in Ranchi, the capital city of Jharkhand. The motive behind the murder was the wife's extramarital affair with another man.

The deceased was identified as Dharmendra Kumar. His wife, Priyanka Devi, was having an affair with a man named Sonu Kumar. Priyanka and Sonu allegedly conspired together to kill Dharmendra. They carried out their plan, resulting in Dharmendra's death. The police have arrested both Priyanka Devi and Sonu Kumar in connection with the murder.

89. NEWS URL: https://t.co/jtAEdizluv

This incident occurred in Meerut, Uttar Pradesh, where a woman, in collusion with her boyfriend, electrocuted her husband to death. The motive behind the murder was rooted in the wife's extramarital affair and her desire to eliminate her husband to continue her relationship with her lover. To cover up the crime, they attempted to stage the death as a result of a snakebite.

The truth came to light when the husband's mobile phone, which was still active, was tracked to Mathura. Upon investigation, authorities discovered inconsistencies in the wife's statements and gathered evidence pointing towards foul play. Subsequently, both the woman and her boyfriend were arrested and charged with the murder. The case highlights the lengths to which individuals may go to pursue illicit relationships, leading to tragic consequences.

90. In Mathura, Uttar Pradesh, a gruesome murder took place on January 19, 2025, in a colony near the highway, where Arti, a 34-year-old woman, and her lover, Pushpendra, killed her 38-year-old husband, Vinod. The duo drugged Vinod with bhang-laced pakoras, strangled him, and then electrocuted his body to disguise the murder as an accident. Initially, Arti misled Vinod's family, who performed his last rites believing it was a natural death, but the crime was uncovered when police traced suspicious mobile phone activity, leading to Arti's confession.

The motive stemmed from Arti's four-year extramarital affair with Pushpendra, which Vinod had discovered, leading to frequent disputes. Determined to eliminate Vinod, who was an obstacle to their relationship, Arti and Pushpendra meticulously planned the murder. The police investigation, triggered by mobile records and inconsistencies in Arti's account, revealed the chilling details, resulting in the arrest of both accused. The case shocked the community, exposing a calculated betrayal driven by infidelity.

91. NEWS URL: https://t.co/XZyMhwHY8i

In Dewas, Madhya Pradesh, a brutal murder occurred on November 24, 2021, along the Dewas-Bhopal road, where Rachna Dhurve, aged 25, and her lover, Anil Saryam, aged 27, killed her husband, Neeraj Parte, a 28-year-old patwari. Anil, enraged by Rachna's recent marriage to Neeraj, befriended him and lured him to a dhaba under the pretense of a meal. There, Anil got Neeraj drunk, killed him with a sharp weapon, and dumped his body under a culvert. On January 30, 2025, both Rachna and Anil were sentenced to life imprisonment by the First District and Additional Sessions Judge for their roles in the planned murder.

The motive stemmed from Anil's anger over Rachna's marriage to Neeraj, which occurred just 20 days before the murder, disrupting their illicit relationship. Rachna, complicit in the plot, supported Anil's plan to eliminate Neeraj, who had become an obstacle to their affair. Police investigations, triggered by the discovery of Neeraj's bloodied body and call records, confirmed Rachna's involvement, leading to their arrests. The case shocked the community, highlighting a deadly conspiracy driven by jealousy and betrayal.

92. This incident occurred in the district court of Dewas, Madhya Pradesh, during the sentencing of the accused. The motive behind the murder was an illicit relationship between the deceased's wife and another man.

The deceased was a Patwari (a land record officer). His wife, Manisha, was having an affair with a man named Narendra. They conspired together and murdered the Patwari. Following the investigation and trial, the court sentenced both Manisha and Narendra to life imprisonment for their crime.

93. NEWS URL: https://t.co/8mbRzFmixA

In Mumbai, Maharashtra, a drug smuggling incident led to the arrest of a 30-year-old woman from West Bengal on January 30, 2025, at Chhatrapati Shivaji Maharaj International Airport. The woman, whose identity was not disclosed, was apprehended by the Air Intelligence Unit (AIU) of Mumbai Customs after arriving from Bangkok. She was found carrying approximately 1 kg of hydroponic weed, valued at Rs 1 crore, concealed in her luggage. The seizure occurred during a routine check, and a case was registered under the NDPS Act, with ongoing investigations to trace the drug trafficking network.

The incident was driven by the woman's alleged involvement in an international drug smuggling operation, motivated by the high profitability of trafficking hydroponic weed, a potent cannabis variant. The act was not directed at a specific individual but was an attempt to illegally supply drugs to the Indian market. The woman acted alone in this instance, though authorities suspect links to a larger syndicate. Her arrest disrupted a significant smuggling attempt, and the case highlights ongoing efforts to curb drug trafficking through Mumbai's international airport.

94. This incident occurred in Mumbai, specifically in the Kurla area. The reason behind the arrest was the possession of a significant quantity of drugs, valued at ?1 crore.

The individual apprehended was a 40-year-old woman. She was found to be in possession of 1 kg of MDMA (methylenedioxymethamphetamine), a banned narcotic substance. The Anti-Narcotics Cell

(ANC) of the Mumbai Police acted on specific information and laid a trap, leading to the woman's arrest. The investigation is currently underway to determine the source of the drugs and the intended recipients.

95. NEWS URL: https://t.co/7zweObzp9Q

In Mathura, Uttar Pradesh, a chilling murder occurred on January 19, 2025, in a colony near the highway, where Arti, a 34-year-old woman, and her lover, Pushpendra, killed her 38-year-old husband, Vinod. Arti fed Vinod bhang-laced parathas to sedate him, then, with Pushpendra's help, strangled him and electrocuted his body to disguise the murder as an accident. Initially, Arti deceived Vinod's family, who performed his last rites believing it was a natural death, but suspicious WhatsApp chats with Pushpendra found on her phone led to a police investigation and her confession.

The motive was driven by Arti's four-year extramarital affair with Pushpendra, which Vinod had discovered, resulting in frequent disputes. Determined to eliminate Vinod, who was an obstacle to their relationship, Arti and Pushpendra planned the murder. The police, acting on mobile evidence and family suspicions, arrested both Arti and Pushpendra, registering a case for further investigation. The case shocked the community, revealing a calculated act of betrayal fueled by infidelity

96. This incident occurred in Mathura, Uttar
Pradesh, where a woman named Rekha conspired
with her lover, Sonu, to murder her husband,
Rakesh. The motive behind the crime was Rekha's
extramarital affair with Sonu, which Rakesh had
discovered. To eliminate Rakesh and continue their
relationship without hindrance, Rekha and Sonu
planned his murder.

On the day of the incident, Rekha prepared parathas
laced with bhaang (a cannabis-based intoxicant) and
served them to Rakesh, rendering him unconscious.
Once incapacitated, Sonu entered the house and
strangled Rakesh to death. The crime came to light
during the police investigation, leading to the arrest
of both Rekha and Sonu. The case highlights the
tragic consequences of illicit relationships and the
lengths individuals may go to pursue forbidden love.

97. This incident occurred in the village of Nagla
Birbal in the Shergarh area of Mathura district, Uttar
Pradesh. The motive behind the murder was the
wife's extramarital affair with another man.

The deceased was identified as 35-year-old Charan
Singh. His wife, Pooja, was having an affair with a
man named Vikas. Pooja and Vikas allegedly
conspired to kill Charan Singh so they could be
together. They carried out their plan by giving
Charan Singh parathas laced with 'bhaang'
(cannabis). Once he was unconscious, they strangled
him to death. The police have arrested both Pooja
and Vikas in connection with the murder.

98. NEWS URL: https://t.co/pBly3QacTm

In Muzaffarpur, Bihar, a heart-wrenching incident occurred on January 29, 2025, in the Brahmpura police station area, where an unidentified woman abandoned her newborn baby on the roadside near the Muzaffarpur-Gorakhpur railway line. The baby, found crying by a patrolling police constable, Shivshankar Kumar, was rescued and admitted to a hospital for medical care. The woman, described as a "Kalyugi mother" in local reports, fled the scene, and her identity remains unknown as police continue their search.

The motive behind the abandonment is unclear, but such acts are often linked to social stigma, poverty, or personal distress, though no specific reason was confirmed in this case. The act was directed at the helpless newborn, who was left vulnerable on the road. Constable Shivshankar Kumar's compassionate response saved the child's life, and he expressed a desire to adopt the baby.

99. NEWS URL: https://t.co/hjCH0C7fG6

This incident occurred in Bhagalpur, Bihar, where a woman and her daughter were involved in an illicit relationship with the same man. Upon discovering this, the woman's husband confronted her, leading to frequent quarrels. To eliminate the obstacle to their affair, the woman, her daughter, and the lover conspired to murder the husband. They killed him and buried his body to conceal the crime.

The murder came to light when suspicious activities were noticed, prompting an investigation. Authorities uncovered the illicit relationships and the conspiracy behind the husband's disappearance. All three accused were arrested and charged with murder.

100. This disturbing incident occurred in the state of West Bengal, although the specific district or town is not mentioned in the headline. The motive behind the murder was a complex and unusual relationship dynamic involving the victim's wife, daughter, and another individual.

The deceased was the head of the household. His wife and daughter were reportedly both in a relationship with the same person. All three individuals – the wife, the daughter, and the shared partner – allegedly collaborated to murder the head of the household. After committing the crime, they buried the body to conceal their actions. The headline indicates that the police have likely uncovered this crime, given the report of the murder and burial.

101. The incident occurred in Meerut, Uttar Pradesh, where a woman named Ravita and her lover, Amardeep, conspired to murder her husband, Amit, a 25-year-old laborer. On a Saturday night, after Amit had dinner and gone to bed, the duo strangled him while he was asleep. To mislead investigators and avoid suspicion, they placed a live snake beside Amit's body and informed others in the village that he had died due to a snake bite. However, suspicions grew, and a post-mortem was conducted, which determined the cause of death to be strangulation,

not envenomation. Following the autopsy results, the police arrested Ravita and Amardeep, who are currently in custody and facing murder charges.

The motive behind the murder appears to be an extramarital affair between Ravita and Amardeep. By eliminating Amit, they aimed to continue their relationship without hindrance. The attempt to disguise the murder as a snakebite was a calculated move to divert attention from their involvement. This case highlights the lengths to which individuals may go to conceal their crimes and the importance of thorough forensic investigations in uncovering the truth.

A Call for Gender-Neutral Justice

The legal and societal framework in India, however, often tends to paint women primarily as victims. This gender-biased narrative, supported by certain NGOs and government ministries, overlooks the growing number of instances where women are perpetrators. This creates a dangerous precedent where gender, rather than the nature of the crime, becomes the basis of legal sympathy and judicial leniency.

Justice should be blind to gender and rooted in evidence, law, and fairness. When a woman commits a crime, she must be held to the same standards of accountability as a man. Whether it is a case of a false dowry complaint, custodial abuse of a child during matrimonial disputes, or participation in organized criminal activity, the rule of law must prevail uniformly. Exempting women from scrutiny or punishment due to their gender not only undermines justice but also erodes the principle of equality before the law.

Recognizing that women are capable of both virtue and vice is essential in creating a truly just society. Crime is not the domain of one gender; it is a human failing. Thus, our legal system must evolve toward a gender-neutral model where punishment is based on the crime committed, not the sex of the offender. Only then can we hope to establish a balanced and credible justice system for all citizens.

Gender-neutral punishment is essential for a just society. The Indian legal system, while striving for fairness, sometimes exhibits leniency toward women, influenced by societal biases or advocacy groups. For instance, women convicted of serious crimes may receive lighter sentences or be granted bail more readily than men in similar cases. This disparity undermines the principle that punishment should reflect the severity of the crime, not the gender of the offender. A murder committed by a woman should carry the same weight as one committed by a man. Similarly, cases of abuse or fraud should be judged on evidence and impact, not on assumptions about gender roles.

In conclusion, acknowledging crimes by Indian women is not about vilifying them but about recognizing their agency—both for good and ill. Women's NGOs and ministries must evolve beyond blanket defenses and advocate for true equality, where accountability is paramount. Justice should be blind to gender, ensuring that punishment fits the crime. Only then can India build a legal and social framework that respects individual responsibility and upholds fairness for all.

Here, we documented around 101 crimes by women of 2025, List is long—most were cold-blooded murders of their husbands. The tactics were calculated and devious, all to clear the path for their extramarital affairs. The conclusion is ugly but obvious: these women didn't kill for money—they killed for lust or to hide their ill deeds or crimes.

According to data compiled by *MyNation Hope Foundation* from mainstream media, more than 600+ husbands are murdered annually by their wives in India. These reports are accessible on Twitter under hashtags **#CrimesByIndianWomen** or **#CrimesByBharatKiLaxmi**, curated over the past four years by activist Aman Kumar from Patna for the NGO *MyNation Hope Foundation*, via his Twitter handle https://twitter.com/mynation_BH

Men are not merely complaining; Men are victims of atrocities by women, supported by verifiable evidence for the judiciary and government. These news reports, publicly available and not authored by us, can be independently searched (We also provided URL for some of these crimes), which are published on main stream media, news channels. Unlike some women's organizations, we don't rely on fabricated data to seek funding. The 600+ reported husband murders are just the tip of the iceberg, with the actual number likely over five times higher. While NCRB reports around 6,000 dowry deaths annually, recent media coverage of such cases is scarce, not a single news report in 2025, revealing a truth some women's organizations may be suppressing while obstructing relief for men.

CHAPTER 9

WARNING TO BACHELORS

In the age-old Indian tradition, marriage has been considered a sacred bond—a union of two souls meant to endure life's ups and downs with mutual love, trust, and respect. For generations, men have grown up dreaming of a happy family life, believing that marriage will bring emotional fulfillment and companionship. However, the reality in modern India is shifting, and the romantic ideals associated with marriage are facing a harsh, sometimes dangerous, contradiction.

Today, many Indian men find themselves trapped in legal, emotional, and financial turmoil soon after marriage. The assumption that every woman entering a marriage does so with pure intentions is increasingly being questioned. There is a growing concern that some women are using marriage not as a bond of love but as a transaction—a means to financial security, social elevation, or even legal revenge.

False dowry harassment cases under Section 498A, false domestic violence complaints, and quick claims for maintenance are being reported with alarming frequency. Shockingly, there are cases where women have filed such claims within days or weeks of the wedding, raising questions about their real intent. This misuse of gender-biased laws has left many innocent men and their families shattered, socially stigmatized, and financially drained.

Worse still, there are chilling reports of pre-marital affairs continuing covertly even after marriage. In such situations, the husband—often unaware—is merely a stepping stone, chosen for his wealth or status. In extreme cases, there have been allegations and investigations pointing to women plotting their husbands' deaths, staging them as accidents or medical tragedies. The motive? To inherit assets and eliminate the legal bond, thereby reuniting with their lovers without consequence.

While these incidents may not represent the majority of Indian marriages, the trend is disturbing enough to warrant serious caution. The laws, as they currently stand, offer limited protection to men, making it crucial for bachelors to be alert and well-informed before taking the marital plunge.

Financial Exploitation: A concerning trend involves marriages motivated by financial gain rather than affection. Some women enter marriages seeking wealth or stability, and reports of false dowry or domestic violence cases filed shortly after marriage are increasing. These cases aim to claim significant maintenance or alimony, draining a man's resources and causing emotional distress. The misuse of protective laws turns marriage into a tool for exploitation.

Deceit and Infidelity: Another troubling issue is undisclosed premarital affairs, where women marry without love, maintaining outside relationships due to societal or familial pressure. In extreme cases, this can lead to dangerous schemes, including orchestrating the husband's death to inherit assets. Though rare, these instances highlight the risks of misplaced trust.

Protecting Yourself: This isn't about portraying all women negatively but urging Indian bachelors to exercise prudence.

Know Your Partner: Before committing, understand your partner's values, aspirations, and character through open communication about expectations, finances, and life goals to identify potential red flags.

- **Verify Background**: Without invading privacy, verify your partner's background for clarity and peace of mind.
- **Seek Advice**: Consult trusted friends, family, or professionals for guidance.
- **Legal Safeguards**: Men should also take legal precautions:

Understand marriage laws.
- Maintain clear financial boundaries.
- Document agreements, such as prenuptial arrangements (where culturally acceptable).
- Trust your instincts and investigate anything that feels amiss before committing to marriage.

WE WARNED YOU

Indian marriages, idealized as sacred unions promising lifelong love and companionship, can present alarming realities for men today. While many Indian men dream of finding a virtuous partner, they must approach marriage with heightened awareness and caution. Although most women seek genuine relationships, disturbing trends necessitate vigilance to protect against emotional, financial, and physical harm.

Marriage is no longer a guaranteed path to happiness and stability for Indian men. It is essential for bachelors to approach the institution of marriage not just with love and optimism but also with awareness and legal foresight. Background checks, pre-nuptial agreements, and honest conversations about expectations and values are not signs of mistrust—they are shields of self-preservation in an increasingly unpredictable marital landscape. Love may be blind, but today, blindness can be fatal.

While marriage can be a beautiful journey with the right partner, blind optimism is risky. Indian bachelors must balance hope with caution, approaching marriage with open eyes to navigate modern relationship complexities and build a future based on trust, respect, and genuine love.

In India, several cases have revealed clever, shocking, and disturbing methods used by some women to murder their husbands or partners—often with the intent to make it look like an accident, natural death, or someone else's crime. Here are some of the most calculated strategies used:

Here's a **summary table** of the various methods used by some Indian women in husband murders, showcasing the **strategy, method used, and intent to cover up**:

Method	Tools/Technique Used	Cover-Up Strategy
Snakebite Murder	Venomous snake (cobra/krait)	Claimed accidental snakebite
Burning After Sedation	Sleeping pills + fire/gas leak	Staged house fire or gas accident
Contract Killing	Lover or hired killer	Faked robbery or random attack
Slow Poisoning	Arsenic, pesticides, crushed glass	Appeared as illness or organ failure
Fake Identity/Body Swap	Burned or disfigured unknown body	Claimed it was husband's body
Electrocution	Live wires in bathroom/taps	Claimed electrical accident
Staged Road Accidents	Drugging + vehicle crash	Declared as traffic accident
Domestic Violence Attack	Blunt tools, boiling oil, gas cylinders	Claimed self-defense or sudden rage

These methods often involved careful planning and misuse of common domestic or rural conditions to **mislead investigators** and **avoid suspicion**.

1. **Snakebite Murders**

As mentioned earlier, venomous snakes (cobra/krait) were used while the victim slept, simulating accidental death. In multiple cases (Kerala, Meerut), the idea was to stage a natural wildlife hazard.

2. **Burning After Sedation**

In several cases, women mixed sleeping pills in food or drinks and, once the husband was unconscious, set them on fire or burned the house down to erase evidence. The aim was to show it as an accidental fire or gas leak.

3. **Hiring a Contract Killer**

In both rural and urban cases, women have:

- Hired their lovers or local criminals to carry out the murder.
- Paid or promised marriage to men in exchange for the killing.

These are often staged as robberies gone wrong or roadside accidents.

4. **Poisoning Over Time**

Slow poisoning using:

- Arsenic
- Pesticides
- Crushed glass

was used to simulate illness or organ failure, fooling even doctors unless a toxicology test was done.

5. **Fake Identity & Swap Murders**

In one Hyderabad case, a woman and her lover killed a homeless person, burned the body beyond recognition, and claimed it was the husband. DNA and tattoo analysis later exposed the truth.

6. **Electrocution**

Women in some cases used live wires in bathrooms or near metal water taps to electrocute husbands, staging it as a freak accident due to faulty wiring.

7. **Staged Road Accidents**

Drugging the husband and staging vehicular accidents is another tactic, especially with help from accomplices. These were initially treated as tragic traffic mishaps.

8. **Domestic Violence Turned Fatal**

In many cases, women used household fights as cover for premeditated attacks—hitting husbands

with grinding stones, gas cylinders, or boiling oil—
and later claimed it was self-defense or sudden rage.

These acts are tragic and extreme outliers, not the
norm. They often stem from deep-seated personal
issues, extramarital affairs, or ongoing abuse (real or
perceived). But they highlight how criminal planning
can exploit social assumptions and everyday tools to
escape detection.

⚠ Warning to Readers: A Reality Check, Not a Generalization

This publication contains references to real incidents
of women involving misuse of marriage laws, false
allegations, and even extreme cases involving the
planning or execution of crimes, forced/harassed to
commit suicide, murders with the help of lovers,
relatives and sometimes themselves. These are not
fictional stories, not exaggerations, and not hearsay.
These stories are not fabricated, exaggerated, or
based on rumours. Each example has been sourced
from actual news reports, legal records, and cases
covered by mainstream Indian media.

We want to be very clear:
**This is not a blanket accusation against all
women.**
We recognize that some women are genuine victims
of abuse and deserve full protection under the law.
But it is equally important to acknowledge that **not
all women are victims** and that many **misuse the**

law for personal or financial gain, often with devastating consequences for innocent men and their families.

However, it is important to clarify that our intention is not to paint all women with the same brush. We do not claim that all women are manipulative, criminal-minded, or capable of harming their partners. Such sweeping generalizations would be unfair and irresponsible.

Our purpose is to challenge the commonly held narrative that women are always victims in marital disputes. What we are exposing is the other side of the coin—where many women misuse legal provisions, manipulate emotional and financial systems, or even go to dangerous lengths for personal gain and eliminate husband/Partner.

Recognizing this reality is not misogyny—it is a necessary step toward creating a fairer, more balanced legal and social framework where both men and women are treated with equal accountability and justice.

The purpose of presenting these facts is not to spread fear or hatred, but to **inform**, **warn**, and **prepare** Indian men—especially bachelors—about the potential legal and emotional risks in today's matrimonial landscape. In a system where certain laws are heavily gender-biased, awareness can be the first line of defense.

We advocate for balanced gender justice, where rights and protections are not granted on the basis of gender alone, but on the basis of truth and evidence.

Let this serve as a caution—not a condemnation. Be informed. Be careful. Be fair.

Ignore this at your own risk. You've been warned.

CHAPTER 10

In India, women are always portrayed as victims—no matter how many crimes they commit or how many men they murder. The reality is buried under a system rigged by culture, society, and a biased mindset. Women's organizations work tirelessly to suppress news about female criminals, shielding them from accountability. This book exposes some of the most brutal crimes committed by Indian women—stories the mainstream refuses to touch.

Meanwhile, lawmakers jump to create new laws overnight if a woman is harmed, but when over 600 men—most of them husbands—are murdered by women each year, the same leaders play dead. Politicians keep one eye open only when it serves women because they are a reliable vote bank. Crores of rupees are poured into so-called "women welfare" schemes, but no one dares to ask where the money actually goes. The answer's obvious, Everyone knows the answer—just look at the ministers' flashy cars, ever-growing assets, and designer clothes that change every hour. That's where all the money goes.

HOW IT STARTED.

Renuka Chaudhary , a former Indian Union Minister for Women and Child Development and Congress politician. The statement, "It's not such a bad idea, except that I have such pity for men," was made during a 2006 interview with Karan Thapar on Devil's Advocate (CNN-IBN) when discussing the

Protection of Women from Domestic Violence Act, 2005, which she helped introduce. The full context involves Thapar asking if men should suffer due to potential misuse of the law before amendments are considered, to which she responded, "That's not a bad idea, except that I have such pity for men." She's also quoted saying, "It's time for men to suffer," in relation to the Act's implementation, as noted in various sources. These remarks have been widely circulated and criticized, especially in recent years, for their perceived insensitivity toward men.

Context of the Statement

Domestic Violence Act, 2005: As Minister (2006–2009), Chowdhury championed this law to protect women from domestic abuse, including physical, emotional, and economic violence. The Act allows women to seek protection orders, maintenance, and residence rights, but critics argue it's prone to misuse due to vague definitions and lack of gender-neutral provisions.

Interview with Karan Thapar: Thapar challenged Chowdhury on the Act's potential for false cases, citing data that 98% of anti-dowry law cases (Section 498A) in 2005 were deemed false. He asked if she was willing to let men suffer before addressing misuse. Her response, "It's not such a bad idea, except that I have such pity for men," was paired with laughter, which critics found dismissive. She also said, "Any law is better than no law at all when protecting women is concerned," defending the Act's necessity despite flaws.

Maneka Gandhi's statement, "All violence is male-generated," made during a 2017 NDTV Walk the Talk interview, stirred significant controversy. As the then-Minister for Women and Child Development, she argued that men are the primary source of violence, stating, "All the violence is male-generated. Every bit of it, even if it's a woman doing it, it's male-generated. The violence comes from men." Her intent was to highlight patriarchal structures as the root of societal violence, including domestic abuse, rape, and broader aggression, suggesting that even women's violent actions stem from male-driven societal conditioning or provocation.

Data Contradictions: While men dominate violent crime statistics (e.g., 95% of violent crime accused in India were male, per 2017 NCRB data), women's involvement (4.8% of cases) shows violence isn't exclusively male-driven.

Broader Implications

Gender and Violence: Gandhi's statement reflects radical feminist views that patriarchy drives societal issues, but it overlooks cases where women act violently without clear male influence (e.g., Priyadarshini's assault or historical examples like female-led crimes).

Cultural Norms: The statement ties into Indian debates about gender roles, where women's actions are judged harshly, often to reinforce traditional expectations. Gandhi's focus on male-driven violence challenges these norms but risks oversimplification.

Policy Context: As a minister, Gandhi pushed for stronger laws against gender-based violence (e.g., amending POCSO Act), but her statement was seen by critics as undermining balanced policy discourse.

Similarly, recently NCP-SP leader Rohini Khadse urges President Murmu, that women should be allowed to commit one murder without punishment.

Against the backdrop of International Women's Day, Nationalist Congress Party (Sharad Pawar's) (NCP)(SP) women's wing on Saturday (March 8, 2025), urged President Droupadi Murmu to allow women to commit one murder, without any punishment in view of the growing crime against women.

While Khadse's frustration over the increasing crimes against women is understandable, advocating for legalized violence is deeply problematic. Such proposals undermine the rule of law and can lead to a breakdown of societal order. Granting individuals the right to commit murder without consequence devalues human life and sets a dangerous precedent. Addressing crimes against women requires strengthening legal frameworks, ensuring swift justice, and promoting societal change, rather than endorsing acts of violence.

Lately, Justice Dr Neela Gokhale said that Section 498A IPC has not been misused but misunderstood by everyone. The judge was speaking at an "interactive lecture" organised by the Interactive Lawyers Association for Women (ILAW) on the topic "Use and Misuse of Section 498A."

The judge stated that while section 498A may be misused by a very handful women but that cannot be used to "paint the entire drawing board in one colour."

"I can say that section 498A is not misused but it is misunderstood by everyone. But it's time, we as the Bar and the Bench must rise to the ocassion and give proper advice to our clients," she said.

If that's the case, why is the conviction rate in 498A cases barely 10%? And why do many women withdraw their 498A complaints once they've received the amount of money they demanded?

Judge admit there are few women misuse 498A, if so why no Women is charged for misusing Section 498A IPC?

All these public statements, support and promote false cases.

Victimhood

Whatever the motive behind statements like "All violence is male-generated" or "It's time for men to suffer," they send a dangerous message to the public. These remarks not only distort reality but also empower opportunists to exploit the system. In Indian society, women receive excessive appeasement—no matter what they do, they're often excused as Abla nari, weak, helpless, or victims of circumstances, even when they commit serious crimes. But a crime is a crime. Justice must be blind and equal for all—not selective based on gender.

Get away Playing Victim

Instances of Abuse and Public Humiliation of Men by Women:

Domestic Violence: Studies indicate that men in India do experience domestic violence, including physical, emotional, and economic abuse, at the hands of their partners or female family members. However, this is often underreported due to social stigma and the perception that men should be strong and not victims.

Public Shaming and Mockery: While less documented in widespread media, instances of men being publicly shamed, ridiculed, or mocked by women can occur in personal or community settings. These incidents might not always escalate to physical violence but can cause significant emotional distress.

False Accusations: There have been reported cases where men have been falsely accused of crimes like harassment or domestic violence, leading to public scrutiny, damage to reputation, and legal battles. The Nisha Sharma case (2003) is a prominent example where the initial portrayal was of a woman standing against dowry, but later, allegations of false accusations emerged.

Physical Altercations: While less common, physical altercations where women are the aggressors and men are victims do occur. These might be isolated incidents or arise in specific social contexts.

Media Glorification - A Complex Issue:

It is uncommon for mainstream media in India to overtly glorify instances where women abuse, publicly beat, or kill men. This is due to several factors:

Prevailing Social Norms: Societal norms often frame men as protectors and women as vulnerable. Media narratives tend to align with these norms.

Legal Frameworks: Laws related to violence and abuse predominantly focus on protecting women, reflecting the historical and ongoing reality of widespread violence against them.

Focus on Women's Empowerment: Media narratives around women often center on empowerment and overcoming oppression. Glorifying violence by women could contradict this narrative.

Sensationalism vs. Glorification: While some incidents of women allegedly perpetrating violence might receive media attention due to their sensational nature, this is usually framed within the context of crime reporting rather than glorification. The focus tends to be on the act itself and the legal consequences, not on celebrating the woman's actions.

Nuances and Potential Interpretations:
Self-Defense: Cases where women use violence against men in self-defense against abuse might be portrayed as acts of bravery and empowerment, but this is distinct from glorifying unprovoked violence.

Misinterpretation of Justice: If a woman takes action against a man she perceives as having wronged her (within or outside the legal system), media coverage might inadvertently be seen by some as glorification, even if the intent is to report on the incident or highlight issues of injustice. However, this is usually accompanied by legal and ethical debates.

Isolated Incidents: While there might be isolated instances in certain cultural or regional contexts where violence by women against perceived wrongdoers is viewed differently, this is not a mainstream media trend.

In conclusion, while men can be victims of abuse and public humiliation by women in India, it is not a common occurrence for the media to glorify such acts. Media attention tends to focus on the legal and social implications of violence, with the dominant narrative still centered on the protection and empowerment of women and many women encash or getaway playing victim.

Indian laws fail to account for the calculated, manipulative ways in which some women eliminate their husbands. These are not impulsive acts—they are often planned with clear motives like Extra marital affairs, property, revenge, or escape from a relationship. This book documents several such disturbing cases, highlighting how men are dying silently while society and the legal system look the other way. If we can term every female death within seven years of marriage as a dowry death, then why not label all male deaths during marriage as potential murders by wives? If justice is truly gender-neutral, then both sides deserve equal scrutiny.

CHAPTER 11

BREVARY AWADS

No one is opposing the government offering special benefits or support schemes for genuinely needy women. However, creating laws exclusively for women—laws that are often misused to exploit loopholes, harass men, and force them into submission—is neither condemned nor questioned by women's ministries, women's organizations, or the government.

Constantly portraying women as victims is unacceptable, especially when there is ample evidence that women are equally capable of committing crimes such as murder, rape, or other serious offenses. Here, we expose some of the most brutal and heinous crimes committed by women. It's up to the reader to decide who truly deserves the bravery awards.

Historical crimes:

Phoolan Devi ("Bandit Queen"): While not solely known for murder, Phoolan Devi led a gang involved in dacoity, kidnapping, and multiple killings, most notably the Behmai massacre where 22 upper-caste men were killed. Her life story is one of extreme violence and social injustice.

Female Gangsters of Mumbai (e.g., Neeta Naik, Jenabai Daruwala): Several women have held significant positions in the Mumbai underworld. Some, like Neeta Naik, were active members of gangs

involved in violence and extortion. Others, like
Jenabai Daruwala, while not directly involved in
violence, wielded considerable influence and
connections within the criminal network.

Seema Parihar: Kidnapped at a young age and
forced into a life of crime, she became a dacoit and
led her own gang, involved in looting, kidnapping,
and murder in the Chambal Valley.

Below is a list of some of the most brutal murders or
crimes committed by Indian women, based on
documented cases from credible media sources,
same can be found on public domain. These cases
are notable for their severity, brutality, or societal
impact. Note that the details are gruesome and may
be disturbing. I've included only verified cases with
clear evidence of female perpetrators, focusing on
murders or violent crimes, as requested. Each case is
presented with factual details and, where applicable,
citations from provided references.

1) **Renuka Shinde and Seema Gavit – Child Murders (1990–1996)**

Details: Sisters Renuka Shinde and Seema Gavit,
along with their mother Anjana Bai, kidnapped 13
children under five years old in Maharashtra to use
them for petty theft and begging. When the children
became uncooperative or problematic, the sisters
brutally murdered them. Methods included hanging
a two-year-old upside down from a pole and banging
a toddler's head against a wall until death. They were
convicted of nine murders, disposing of the bodies
callously.

Brutality: The targeting of defenseless young children and the violent methods used, such as blunt force trauma and strangulation, make these crimes exceptionally horrific.

2) KD Kempamma (Cyanide Mallika) – Serial Killings (1999–2007)

Details: KD Kempamma, known as "Cyanide Mallika," is India's first convicted female serial killer. Between 1999 and 2007, she murdered at least six women in Karnataka by posing as a pious woman at temples. She befriended distressed women, lured them to remote temples under the pretense of performing rituals, and poisoned them with cyanide-laced water or food to steal their jewelry. Her victims included Mamatha Rajan (1999), Elizabeth (2007), and Nagaveni (2007). She was arrested in 2007 after attempting to dispose of stolen jewelry and confessed to the crimes.

Brutality: The methodical use of cyanide to kill vulnerable women and rob them, often after gaining their trust, marks these crimes as particularly cold-blooded.

3) Shabnam Ali – Family Massacre (2008)

Details: Shabnam Ali, along with her lover Saleem, murdered seven members of her family in Amroha, Uttar Pradesh, on April 14, 2008, because her family opposed their relationship. She drugged her parents, two brothers, sister-in-law, cousin, and 10-month-old nephew with sedative-laced milk, after which

Saleem hacked them to death with an axe. Shabnam herself strangled her nephew. The crime was discovered when neighbors reported the bodies.

Brutality: The scale of the massacre—killing seven family members, including a child, in a single night—combined with the use of sedatives and brutal hacking, shocked the nation.

4) Baby Kala – Husband's Murder (2010)

Details: In Chennai, Tamil Nadu, Baby Kala murdered her husband, Radhakrishnan, in 2010 with her lover, Gowri Shankar. The couple, married for 15 years, had frequent quarrels, leading Kala to begin an affair. To eliminate Radhakrishnan, Kala and Shankar killed him (method not specified in sources, likely strangulation or blunt force). Kala confessed to the crime on a Tamil reality TV show in 2014, upset over Shankar's plan to marry another woman.

Brutality: The murder was premeditated, targeting her husband to continue her affair. The public confession on TV added a dramatic twist, exposing the crime years later.

5) Seerat Kaur (2017)

Details: On the night of March 18, 2017, Seerat Kaur, a 35-year-old woman, allegedly shot her 39-year-old husband, Ekam Singh Dhillon, a property dealer, with her licensed 9mm pistol at their rented first-floor residence in Phase 3B1, Mohali. The couple had a strained relationship for years, exacerbated by ongoing disputes. After killing him, Seerat bundled Ekam's body into a suitcase, intending to dispose of it. The body was placed in the boot of Ekam's BMW car outside their home.

Brutality: The murder involved a point-blank gunshot to Ekam's head, with the bullet exiting through his left temple. Ekam, who was 6 feet 3 inches tall and weighed over 100 kg, was stuffed into a 3.5-foot suitcase, a task that required significant effort. The act of packing and attempting to dispose of the body underscores the calculated nature of the crime.

Discovery: The crime came to light on March 19, 2017, when an unidentified auto-rickshaw driver reported seeing blood oozing from a suitcase while assisting a woman (Seerat) in placing it into the BMW's boot. Scared, he fled and alerted the police. Officers recovered Ekam's body from the suitcase outside the couple's home (House No. 116, Phase 3B1). Seerat and her family had fled by then, leaving their two children (a 10-year-old son and a 6-year-old daughter) at home.

6) Jolly Joseph (2002-2016)

Details: This woman from Kerala was arrested in 2019 for allegedly orchestrating the deaths of six family members over 14 years. The deaths, which occurred between 2002 and 2016, were initially believed to be from natural causes, but suspicion arose and investigations revealed the presence of cyanide in some of the victims' bodies.

7) Bandana Kalita – Double Murder and Dismemberment (2023)

Details: In Guwahati, Assam, Bandana Kalita murdered her husband, Amarjyoti Dey, and her mother-in-law, Shankari Dey, in 2023, with help from her lover. She choked and killed them, dismembered their bodies, stored the parts in a refrigerator, and dumped them across Meghalaya over months. She filed a false missing persons report to cover up the crime, which was uncovered when neighbors reported a foul smell.

Brutality: The act of dismembering and storing body parts, coupled with the prolonged disposal, mirrors high-profile cases like Shraddha Walkar's murder, but received less media attention.

8) Suchana Seth – Child Murder (2024)

Details: Suchana Seth, a Bengaluru-based startup CEO, murdered her four-year-old son in a hotel room in Goa in January 2024, reportedly due to a custody dispute with her husband, Venkat Raman. She smothered the child, hid his body in a suitcase, and attempted to transport it to Karnataka by taxi. Blood-stained towels in the hotel room alerted staff, leading to her arrest in Chitradurga.

Brutality: The murder of her own young child and the attempt to conceal the body in a suitcase highlight the calculated and gruesome nature of the crime.

9) Befriending and Poisoning Gang (Andhra Pradesh): In September 2024, three women were arrested in Andhra Pradesh for allegedly befriending strangers, offering them cyanide-laced drinks, and then stealing their valuables after they died. They confessed to at least four murders.

10) Suchana Seth – Son's Murder, Husband's Context (2024)

Details: In Goa, Suchana Seth, a Bengaluru-based startup CEO, smothered her four-year-old son in a hotel room in January 2024, amid a custody dispute with her husband, Venkat Raman. While this case primarily involves her son, it's included due to the marital context and reports of strained relations with her husband, whom she allegedly targeted indirectly through the child. She hid the body in a suitcase and was caught while transporting it.

Brutality: Smothering a young child and attempting to conceal the body in a suitcase is deeply shocking. The crime's link to marital discord suggests a broader intent to harm her husband emotionally.

11) Pragati – Husband's Murder (2025)

Details: In Auraiya, Uttar Pradesh, Pragati, a newlywed, orchestrated the murder of her husband, Dilip, a millionaire businessman, just 15 days after their arranged marriage in early 2025. Having an affair with Anurag, Pragati used money from a post-wedding ritual to hire a hitman, who shot Dilip. The motive was to eliminate Dilip and pursue her relationship with Anurag.

Brutality: The speed of the crime—within two weeks of marriage—and the use of a hired killer demonstrate cold calculation. The shooting was swift but planned to ensure Dilip's death.

12) Incident: On April 16, 2025, Rahul and his wife were returning home on a two-wheeler after shopping and dining out. The wife, pretending she dropped her slippers, asked Rahul to stop near ITI College on the Indore-Ichapur highway. As he halted, Yuvraj's two friends ambushed him. The group dragged Rahul off the road, and the wife initiated the attack by striking him with a beer bottle, rendering him unconscious. The juvenile and Lalit then stabbed him 36 times with a broken beer bottle, targeting his neck, chest, arms, and stomach. Rahul died on the spot.

Post-Murder: The wife video-called Yuvraj to show him Rahul's blood-soaked body, reportedly saying, "Kaam ho gaya" (The job is done). The group fled to Raver railway station, took a train to Itarsi, and later headed toward Ujjain.

Brutality: The sheer number of stab wounds (36) and the use of a jagged beer bottle highlight the ferocity of the attack. The premeditated nature, involving luring Rahul to a specific spot, adds to the crime's chilling calculation.

13) Razia Sultana, Uttar Pradesh Murder Case:

Victim: Naushad Ahmad (38), who had recently returned from Dubai.

Accused: His wife, Razia Sultana, her nephew Roman (27), and Roman's friend Himanshu.

Motive: Razia was allegedly having an affair with her nephew, Roman, and her husband, Naushad, found out. They plotted to eliminate him as an obstacle.

Brutality: On the night of April 19-20, 2025, Razia allegedly sedated Naushad. Roman and Himanshu then arrived, and the trio strangled him. They subsequently dismembered his body using sharp-edged tools to fit it into a suitcase.

Murders in brief
In recent months, several cases of Indian women murdering their husbands have gained media attention:

Auraiya, Uttar Pradesh: A 22-year-old woman, Pragati Yadav, and her lover hired a contract killer to murder her husband just two weeks after their marriage because they were unable to meet. They paid the killer, Ramaji Chaudhary, Rs 2 lakh to commit the murder. She was reportedly still in love with someone else and unhappy with the marriage.

Jaipur, Rajasthan: A woman named Gopali Devi, along with her lover, murdered her husband, Dhannalal Saini, after he discovered their affair.

They attempted to dispose of the body by setting it on fire.

Meerut: Muskan Rastogi, along with her lover, murdered her husband, Saurabh, and stuffed his body in a drum with cement and salt. She had drugged him with sleeping pills before killing him.

Rudrapur, Udham Singh Nagar district: Parul Singh and her lover, Mohammad Raees Hussain, were arrested for murdering her husband, Harish Kumar. They suffocated him with a pillow and dumped his body in a wheat field.

Mathura: Poonam Kumari was sentenced to life in prison for murdering her differently-abled husband with the help of her teenage lover.

Madhya Pradesh: A woman killed her husband and showed his body to her lover on a video call

Madhya Pradesh (April 2025): As you mentioned, a 17-year-old wife allegedly conspired with her lover and others to murder her 25-year-old husband. The motive appears to be to be with her lover.

Belagavi, Karnataka (December 2024): A woman was arrested for allegedly killing her husband, who she claimed was a drunkard and abusive, especially regarding her property. She reportedly strangled him, smashed his face with a stone, and then cut his body into pieces to dispose of it.

MEDIA TRIALS

1) Nisha Sharma is an Indian woman who gained
international attention in 2003 for calling off her
wedding at the last minute, accusing her prospective
groom, Munish Dalal, and his family of demanding
an additional dowry of Rs.1,200,000 (about
US$25,000) and a car. At the time, she was a 21-
year-old software engineering student in Noida,
India. Her decision to contact the police and file a
complaint under India's anti-dowry laws (IPC 498A)
made headlines, portraying her as a symbol of
resistance against the illegal practice of dowry,
which, despite being banned in India since 1961,
remains prevalent.

Sharma's case received widespread media coverage,
with Indian and global outlets, including The Oprah
Winfrey Show, praising her as a youth icon and role
model for women. The incident was even included in
a Class 6 English textbook in Delhi as an example of
standing up against dowry. However, the case took a
controversial turn when, in 2012, the Gautam Budh
Nagar district court acquitted Dalal, his mother
Vidya Dalal, aunt Savitri Sharma, and another
individual, Navneet Rai, due to insufficient evidence.
The court concluded that Sharma's allegations were
fabricated and her decision to cancel the wedding
was "pre-planned," possibly to avoid marrying Dalal,
as she allegedly had a prior relationship or marriage
with Rai.

The acquittal shifted public perception, with some,
particularly men's rights groups, citing the case as
an example of the misuse of anti-dowry laws. Munish
Dalal claimed the false accusations ruined his

family's reputation, leading to his mother's job loss and social stigma. Sharma faced further scrutiny in 2013 when her sister-in-law, Manisha Sharma, accused her and her brother of dowry harassment, though the outcome of that case is unclear.

According to some reports and the court's observation, Nisha Sharma allegedly fabricated the dowry charges as she wanted to marry someone else. Munish Dalal and his family claimed that Nisha Sharma was already secretly married to another man before her engagement with him.

So, while Nisha Sharma initially brought the issue of alleged dowry demand to the forefront, the subsequent legal proceedings and the court's verdict presented a different perspective on the matter.

2) The Muslim woman from Kerala you're referring to is likely Rehana Fathima, an activist known for her controversial actions challenging social and religious norms. In 2020, she posted a video on social media showing her teenage children painting on her semi-nude body, which sparked significant backlash. The video was part of her artistic and activist expression, aiming to challenge taboos around nudity and promote body positivity, but it was widely criticized as inappropriate, particularly due to the involvement of her children.

The case drew polarized reactions. Some defended her as an advocate for free expression and women's rights, while others, including conservative groups, condemned her actions as morally and legally unacceptable. The involvement of her children intensified the controversy, with critics arguing it was exploitative.

Rehana Fathima has been involved in other high-profile controversies, such as attempting to enter the Sabarimala temple in 2018, defying restrictions on women of menstruating age. Her actions consistently challenge patriarchal and religious norms, making her a polarizing figure.

3) The "Lucknow girl" refers to Priyadarshini Narayan Yadav, a woman who, in a viral video from July 30, 2021, was seen slapping a cab driver, Saadat Ali Siddiqui, over 20 times at Awadh Crossing in Lucknow, Uttar Pradesh. The incident sparked widespread outrage, legal action, and a heated debate on social media, with the hashtag **#ArrestLucknowGirl** trending.

According to reports, Priyadarshini claimed the cab driver nearly hit her while she was crossing the road, alleging he was speeding or jumped a red light. In response, she physically assaulted him, dragging him by the collar, breaking his phone, and allegedly taking Rs.600 from his dashboard. CCTV footage later suggested she was crossing during heavy traffic, and the cab stopped in time, casting doubt on her claim of being hit. The driver, Saadat, did not retaliate and repeatedly asked for police intervention. A traffic constable was present but initially failed to stop the assault. Bystanders recorded the event, and the video went viral, fueling public anger.

The police issued a challan to Saadat and two others for "breach of peace" and let Priyadarshini off with a warning, prompting accusations of bias.

Priyadarshini filed a complaint against Saadat, claiming he tried to run her over. She also alleged prior harassment and showed scars, claiming she'd been beaten in the past.

The driver reported losing self-respect, facing social stigma, and struggling financially due to the incident

4) Hitesha Chandranee and Zomato Delivery Boy (2021)

On March 9, 2021, Hitesha Chandranee, a Bengaluru-based content creator and makeup artist, posted a viral video on Instagram and Twitter alleging that Zomato delivery executive Kamaraj (28) punched her, causing a nasal fracture, after an argument over a delayed food order. She claimed he barged into her Electronic City apartment, verbally abused her, and hit her when she tried to cancel the order. Kamaraj was arrested the next day. However, Kamaraj countered that Hitesha verbally abused him, called him a "slave," and threw slippers at him. He claimed she accidentally hit herself with her ring while he defended himself, causing her nose to bleed. The apartment lacked CCTV, leaving no conclusive evidence.

5) Kanpur Woman Slapping Traffic Cop (2021)

In Kanpur, Uttar Pradesh, a woman was filmed slapping a traffic policeman during a roadside argument over a traffic violation. The video, widely shared on Twitter/X and covered by Zee News, showed her verbally abusing and physically striking the officer while a crowd watched. The incident stemmed from her refusal to show vehicle documents.

6) Ghaziabad Society Argument: In August 2022, a video circulated widely showing a heated argument in a residential society in Ghaziabad, near Delhi, where a woman was seen behaving aggressively towards a security guard and other residents. Reports suggested the argument was over some society rules. While the video showed aggressive behavior, it's important to note that the full context and the reasons for the altercation might be more complex. Media coverage focused on the public confrontation and the woman's behavior.

7) Gurugram Road Rage Incident: In 2023, a video reportedly from Gurugram (near Delhi) showed a woman confronting and allegedly slapping a man in his car during a road rage incident. The video sparked debate online about who was at fault and the appropriateness of the woman's actions.

8) Agra Woman Beating Security Guard (2022): A video surfaced of a woman in Agra beating a security guard with sticks and abusing him verbally. X user posted on Twitter noted, "Videos with women beating & abusing men going viral almost daily," but highlighted no action by police.

9) Noida Woman Slapping Rickshaw Driver (2022): Another viral video showed a woman slapping a rickshaw driver 17 times in 45 seconds.

10) Wife Beating Husband with Bats (2022): Twitter user shared a viral video of a woman beating her husband with bats, noting, "This woman is SCOT FREE. Never saw a single day of jail"

11) Delhi Woman Abusing Metro Staff (2023)

A woman was recorded verbally abusing and physically pushing Delhi Metro staff after a dispute over ticketing. The video, shared on Twitter/X and covered by India Today, showed her mocking the staff, a male employee, in front of passengers.

12) Bengaluru Woman Killing Husband (2023)

In Bengaluru, a woman named Anusha killed her husband, Mahesh, by poisoning him during a domestic dispute. The case, reported by The Indian Express, gained attention due to Anusha's claim of enduring years of physical abuse. The murder occurred at home but was widely covered due to its domestic violence angle.

13) Mumbai Woman Assaulting Delivery Boy (2023)

A woman in Mumbai was recorded beating a food delivery boy with a slipper and abusing him verbally outside a residential building. The video, shared on Twitter/X and covered by News18, showed her attacking him over a delayed delivery. Bystanders filmed but didn't intervene.

14) Noida Wife and Lover Murdering Husband (2024)

In Greater Noida's Kasna area, Mamta (24) and her lover Bahadur (18) were arrested for murdering Mamta's husband, Bani Singh (26), a security guard. Mamta confessed to stabbing him with a dagger, citing frequent assaults by Singh. The crime was reported on December 14, 2024, after Singh's brother lodged a complaint

15) Hyderabad Woman Abusing Bus Conductor (2024)

In Hyderabad, a woman was filmed verbally abusing and threatening a male bus conductor over a fare dispute. The video, reported by The Hindu, showed her mocking him in front of passengers, with some physical pushing.

In these cases, the media conducted relentless trials, offering continuous coverage that glorified the women's actions—labelling them brave and bold— and catapulting them to instant fame. However, when the truth eventually emerged, the media

distanced itself, and in most instances, no legal
action was taken against the women involved in most
cases. The real victims were the men—who lost their
livelihoods, reputations, and dignity. The Indian
government and its ministers seem focused solely on
glorifying women, but can they ever compensate for
the destroyed lives and restore the names and
reputations of these men?

CHAPTER 12

DOUBLE STANDARD

The Delhi gang rape, also known as the Nirbhaya case, occurred on the night of December 16, 2012, in the Munirka neighborhood of South Delhi.

The victims: A 23-year-old physiotherapy intern, referred to as Nirbhaya, meaning "fearless", and her male friend, A P Pandey, were returning home after watching a movie.

At approximately 9:30 PM (IST), they boarded a private bus at the Munirka bus stand, heading towards Dwarka. There were six other men on the bus, including the driver.

A scuffle broke out, and the woman's friend was beaten unconscious with an iron rod. The men then dragged Jyoti to the back of the bus and brutally gang-raped her repeatedly for over an hour while the bus continued to drive around Delhi.

After the assault, the attackers robbed both victims. They then attempted to throw them out of the moving bus.

Aftermath:

The Delhi gang rape triggered widespread national and international outrage, leading to significant consequences:

- **Public Protests:** Massive protests erupted across India, with people demanding justice for the victim and increased safety for women. Demonstrators clashed with police in New Delhi, and protests took place in various other cities. Online campaigns also saw widespread participation.

- **Legal Reforms:** The incident led to the formation of a judicial committee to review and suggest amendments to the existing rape laws for quicker investigation and prosecution of sex offenders. This resulted in the **Criminal Law (Amendment) Act, 2013**, also known as the **Anti-rape Act**. Key changes included:

  - Expanding the definition of rape to include other forms of sexual assault.
  - Introducing new offenses like stalking, acid attacks, and voyeurism.
  - Recognizing the mere threat of rape as a criminal act.
  - Increasing the minimum sentence for rape from seven to ten years, and up to 20 years or life imprisonment in cases leading to the victim's death or a vegetative state.
  - Stipulating that the victim's character is irrelevant in rape cases.

- **Establishment of Fast-Track Courts:** To expedite the hearing of rape cases, several fast-track courts were established.
- **Increased Reporting of Crimes:** There was a noticeable increase in the number of women willing to file police reports for sexual assault after the incident, indicating a greater public awareness and willingness to seek justice.
- **Nirbhaya Fund:** The government launched the Nirbhaya Fund to support projects ensuring the safety and security of women.

- **Trial and Conviction:** All six accused were arrested. One of the accused, the bus driver Ram Singh, died in police custody by suicide during the trial. The juvenile accused was tried separately and received the maximum sentence of three years in a reform facility. The remaining four adult accused – Mukesh Singh, Vinay Sharma, Akshay Thakur, and Pawan Gupta – were convicted of rape and murder and sentenced to death by the trial court in September 2013. The Delhi High Court and the Supreme Court upheld their convictions and death sentences. After numerous legal appeals were exhausted, the four men were **executed by hanging on March 20, 2020**, over seven years after the crime.
- **Continued Focus on Women's Safety:** Despite the legal changes and increased awareness, concerns about the safety and security of women in India persist. Activists and the victim's parents have expressed that while some progress has been made, significant gaps in implementation and societal attitudes remain.

Value of Man's Life

According to Indian law, the judiciary, and government, no man has been officially recorded as murdered, killed, or driven to suicide due to harassment by a wife or legal provisions. However, evidence suggests over 600 husbands have been brutally killed or murdered in highly innovative and painful ways, as detailed in our previous murder list.

- **Anything changed for men**? No significant policy or legal changes have been implemented to address male victims of domestic violence or murder by spouses.
- **Any new law drafted for men**? No specific laws have been drafted to protect men from domestic violence or spousal murder.
- **Any legal reform or new law for men**? No notable legal reforms or new laws focus on men's safety in the context of spousal violence.
- **Any fast-track court for men only or NCRB tracking men's deaths**? No fast-track courts exist exclusively for men, and NCRB does not specifically track men's deaths due to spousal murder.
- **Any funding for men**? No dedicated funding, equivalent to the Nirbhaya Fund, exists for men's safety or support.
- **How many women are hanged for murdering their husband**? No records indicate women being hanged for murdering their husbands in India.
- **Any focus on married men's safety**? There is little to no governmental or judicial focus on the safety of married men from spousal violence.

While a single woman's murder can prompt swift legal changes, the deaths of over 600 Indian men annually, brutally killed by their wives—through methods like stabbing 36 times with broken beer bottles, poisoning, running over with vehicles, or throat-slitting—are largely ignored, despite being more gruesome than the Nirbhaya case, where a woman was raped and killed by strangers, but these men are killed by their own most loved and trusted person.

Execution of Women
No Recent Executions of Women for Murder: While the death penalty technically exists for this crime, there have been no executions of women in India for murder in recent history. The last recorded execution of a woman in India was Rattan Bai Jain in 1955

Rattan Bai Jain holds the distinction of being the first woman executed in independent India. She was hanged on 3 January 1955 at Tihar Jail, New Delhi, for the murder of three young girls.

Jain served as the manager of a sterility clinic. Driven by suspicion and jealousy, she poisoned three girls employed at her clinic, believing they were involved in affairs with her husband. Following her arrest, she was tried and convicted for these murders.

No women who murdered their husbands in India have been charged or hanged, highlighting a clear double standard in the legal system. This demonstrates that men's lives are not valued in the Indian legal system.

Unanswered Questions
In India, the brutal murder of a single woman can ignite nationwide outrage, prompting swift legal

reforms and public action. The 2012 Nirbhaya case, where a young woman was gang-raped and murdered by strangers, led to widespread protests, fast-tracked trials, and amendments to India's criminal laws, including harsher penalties for sexual violence. Yet, a starkly different reality exists for the over 600 Indian men who, according to estimates, are brutally killed each year by their wives or intimate partners—often in ways more gruesome than the Nirbhaya case. These deaths, involving methods like stabbing with broken beer bottles, poisoning, running over with vehicles, or throat-slitting, are met with silence, both from society and the state. This disparity reveals a troubling gender bias in how violent crimes are perceived and addressed in India.

The Nirbhaya case, horrific as it was, involved strangers attacking a woman in a public space, violating societal norms of safety and honor. The visceral public reaction stemmed from the collective sense of vulnerability it exposed, particularly for women. In contrast, the murders of men by their wives occur within the private sphere, often by the person they trust most—their spouse. These acts, though equally heinous, are dismissed as isolated incidents or justified under narratives of provocation, such as alleged abuse or infidelity. Unlike the Nirbhaya case, which galvanized legal and social change, these men's deaths rarely make headlines, let alone spark policy discussions. The lack of outrage suggests a societal blind spot: violence against men, especially by women, is not seen as a systemic issue warranting attention.

This double standard is rooted in cultural and legal frameworks that prioritize women's safety over men's. India's laws, such as Section 498A of the Indian Penal Code, are designed to protect women from domestic cruelty, but there are no equivalent protections for men facing similar violence. The assumption that men are inherently stronger or less vulnerable ignores the reality of their victimization. When a woman is killed, it is framed as a national tragedy; when a man is murdered by his wife, it is often trivialized or sensationalized as a personal failing. The gruesome nature of these killings— stabbing a man 36 times or poisoning him slowly— should shock the conscience just as much as Nirbhaya's death did, yet they are met with apathy.

The Indian government's swift response to high-profile women's cases contrasts sharply with its inaction on male victims. Legal reforms post-Nirbhaya included the Criminal Law (Amendment) Act of 2013, which expanded definitions of rape and increased punishments. No comparable measures exist to address intimate partner violence against men, despite the scale of the issue. Over 600 annual deaths, many involving extreme cruelty, should prompt at least an inquiry into the causes and prevention of such crimes. Instead, these cases are buried under societal indifference and a lack of advocacy for male victims.

Addressing this disparity requires acknowledging that violence is not gendered in its capacity to devastate. Both men and women can be victims of horrific crimes, and justice should not depend on the victim's gender. Public campaigns, legal protections, and data collection on male victims are essential steps toward equity. Until society and the state recognize the brutality of these murders with the same urgency as they did Nirbhaya's, the deaths of hundreds of men will continue to be ignored, their stories reduced to mere statistics in a system that fails to see their pain.

The Case for Gender-Blind Justice: Accountability for Selective Laws

The principle of justice demands impartiality, yet India's legal system often leans heavily in favor of women, creating a dangerous imbalance that implicitly condones violence against men. While empowering women through quotas, reservations, or welfare schemes is a separate debate, the law's selective leniency toward women in cases of violent crimes—such as the brutal murders of over 600 men annually by their wives—cannot be justified. When laws, judiciary, or government favor one gender, they bear the blood of the victims on their hands, indirectly encouraging and promoting such crimes by failing to hold women equally accountable.

Justice must be blind, treating every individual—regardless of gender—as equal before the law. However, India's legal framework, including provisions like Section 498A, is designed to protect women from domestic violence, with no comparable safeguards for men facing similar abuse or murder. Cases where men are stabbed, poisoned, run over, or have their throats slit by their wives are often downplayed or met with leniency, with perpetrators receiving lighter sentences or evading scrutiny under narratives of provocation. This selective application of justice signals that men's lives are less valuable, emboldening some women to commit heinous acts without fear of proportional consequences.

The judiciary and government's role in this imbalance is undeniable. By prioritizing women's protection while ignoring male victims, they create a culture where violence against men is normalized or excused. For instance, the swift legal reforms following the 2012 Nirbhaya case demonstrate the state's capacity to act decisively when women are victims. Yet, the gruesome deaths of hundreds of men each year provoke no such urgency, no policy debates, and no public outcry. This double standard not only fails male victims but also perpetuates a system where women are infantilized, presumed incapable of serious wrongdoing, and thus shielded from accountability.

When the law takes sides, it becomes complicit in the crimes it fails to address. By not enacting gender-neutral laws or ensuring equal prosecution, the judiciary and government indirectly endorse a hierarchy of victimhood, where women's suffering is prioritized, and men's is erased. This selective justice fosters resentment and undermines trust in the legal system. If a woman's murder can prompt nationwide reforms, the systematic killing of men should at least warrant investigation and legislative action. Failure to do so makes the state a silent partner in these murders, encouraging their continuation through inaction.

True equality in law requires dismantling gender biases in both legislation and enforcement. Gender-neutral laws, rigorous prosecution of all violent crimes, and public awareness of male victims are critical steps toward justice. Until the law holds everyone accountable equally, the blood of murdered men will stain the hands of those who uphold a system that promotes selective justice, betraying the very principle of fairness it claims to serve.

Other than this Women can acquire husband property even she is accused or accessory to murder. Yes, there is a legal principle in India that a person cannot claim inheritance from someone they murdered, based on the **maxim "Nemo ex suo delicto meliorem suam conditionem facere potest"**, which means "**no one can improve their condition by their own wrongdoing.**" This principle is well-established in Indian law, including in succession matters.

However, in 2024, a Supreme Court of India judgment did make headlines for a nuanced ruling in a case involving a woman who was accused of murdering her husband.

Promotion of Sex and Adultery
On April 15, 2007, during an AIDS awareness event in Delhi, American actor Richard Gere publicly kissed Bollywood actress Shilpa Shetty on the cheek. This act sparked significant controversy in India, leading to protests and legal actions against both actors. While the charges against Gere were quickly dismissed, Shetty faced prolonged legal proceedings. In January 2022, a Mumbai court discharged her from the case, stating she was the victim of Gere's actions.

Kerala, 2017: A 21-year-old woman was arrested in Kottayam district for allegedly sexually abusing a 17-year-old boy. They reportedly met through Facebook and later decided to stay together in an abandoned house. The woman was booked under relevant sections of the Protection of Children from Sexual Offences (POCSO) Act. If its Man then he would have booked under RAPE, Outraging modesty and what not.

Gautami Patil Incident (May 2023): Popular Lavani folk dancer Gautami Patil faced backlash after a video surfaced showing her kissing a young boy on the cheek during a stage performance. In the video, Patil invited the boy to dance with her, attempted to kiss him, and eventually kissed him on the cheek. This act was met with criticism from the public, with many deeming it inappropriate. if Man done this then, he would have booked under various sections of Law.

There have been cases where older women engaged in sexual relationships with teenage boys—some even involving teachers who seduced or eloped with them—yet these women are rarely charged with rape. This reflects a clear bias in the Indian legal system.

All of this not only exposes bias in the legal system but also amounts to the tacit promotion of criminal behavior and Crime.

The Unseen Sacrifices: Honoring Soldiers' Parents Alongside Widows

The narrative surrounding a soldier's sacrifice often centers on his widow, celebrated as a "veer nari" (brave widow), while the profound contributions of his parents are quietly overlooked. When a soldier dies defending India's borders, his widow receives awards, pensions, and public sympathy, but the parents—who birthed, raised, and shaped him into a brave protector—are rarely acknowledged. This disparity reflects a societal and governmental tendency to elevate one form of sacrifice while sidelining another, equally vital, contribution to the nation's heroes.

A poignant example is Smriti Singh, who accepted the Kirti Chakra for her husband, Captain Anshuman Singh, killed in a Siachen fire in 2023. Her grief was broadcast across media, her story resonated widely, and her husband's heroism was rightly celebrated. Smriti, married to Captain Singh for a short time, became the face of his legacy, receiving the nation's honors and support. Yet, Captain Singh's aging parents, who nurtured him for decades, instilling courage and patriotism, were largely absent from the narrative. They bore the labor of raising a son who would defend the nation, only to see his sacrifice symbolized through an award presented to his widow. This oversight diminishes the role of parents, whose lifelong dedication made their son a soldier in the first place.

The focus on widows, while important, often eclipses the parents' silent grief and sacrifice. A soldier's mother and father endure years of anxiety, knowing their child faces mortal danger, and their loss is no less profound when he falls. Unlike widows, who may receive financial aid, job opportunities, or public recognition, parents are rarely afforded similar support or acknowledgment. The Kirti Chakra, a symbol of Captain Singh's valor, rightfully honors his memory, but its presentation to his widow alone underscores a narrow view of who bears the cost of a soldier's sacrifice.

This imbalance calls for a more inclusive approach to honoring fallen soldiers. Recognizing widows is essential, but so is acknowledging the parents who shaped these heroes. Public ceremonies, media narratives, and government policies should highlight the role of parents, ensuring they share in the honors and support extended to widows. Pensions and welfare schemes could be structured to include aging parents, and award ceremonies could invite them to stand alongside widows, reflecting their shared loss.

By focusing solely on the widow, society risks forgetting the roots of a soldier's bravery. Captain Singh's parents, like countless others, deserve recognition for raising a defender of the nation. Honoring them alongside veer naris would affirm that a soldier's sacrifice is a collective legacy, born from the love and labor of all who made him who he was.

The Myth of Patriarchy as a Tool for Gendered Legislation in India

Feminists frequently label India as a patriarchal society, citing systemic male dominance as a justification for women-centric laws and policies. However, the absence of a single law explicitly favoring men, coupled with an abundance of legal protections and appeasements exclusively for women, challenges this narrative. This imbalance raises a critical question: is the claim of patriarchy being weaponized to secure benefits, push for women-centric legislation, and attract government grants, rather than addressing genuine inequities?

In a truly patriarchal system, one would expect laws that explicitly privilege men over women, yet India's legal framework tells a different story. Laws like Section 498A of the Indian Penal Code, which addresses cruelty against married women, the Protection of Women from Domestic Violence Act, 2005, and stringent anti-rape provisions under the Criminal Law (Amendment) Act, 2013, are designed to protect women, with no equivalent safeguards for men facing similar abuses. Dowry laws, maternity benefits, and women-specific welfare schemes further tilt the scales, offering protections and privileges unavailable to men. For instance, while women can claim maintenance after divorce, men rarely receive similar support, even in cases of proven hardship. This one-sided legal landscape undermines the argument that India's system inherently favors men.

The appeasement of women extends beyond laws to societal and governmental practices. Women receive reservations in education, jobs, and politics, such as the 33% quota in local governance and the 2023 Women's Reservation Bill for Parliament. Public transport often includes women-only seats or coaches, and financial schemes like the Mahila Samman Savings Certificate target women exclusively. In contrast, men face mandatory military conscription in some contexts, higher suicide rates, and workplace pressures without corresponding legal or social safety nets. If patriarchy were as dominant as claimed, such overwhelming favoritism toward women would be inexplicable.

This discrepancy suggests that the narrative of patriarchy may serve as a strategic tool. By framing India as a male-dominated society, feminists and advocacy groups can justify demands for more women-centric laws, secure government grants for women's programs, and extract societal benefits. For example, the Ministry of Women and Child Development's budget for 2024–25 allocates billions for women's welfare, including schemes like Beti Bachao Beti Padhao, with no parallel funding for men's issues. The patriarchy narrative amplifies these efforts, portraying women as perpetually oppressed, thus necessitating continuous intervention. This approach risks sidelining men's vulnerabilities, such as the estimated 600 annual murders of men by their wives, which receive little attention compared to violence against women.

However, the issue is not the existence of women's protections but their exclusivity and the lack of gender-neutral alternatives. A balanced legal system would address vulnerabilities across genders, recognizing that men, too, face abuse, discrimination, and societal pressures. The absence of such laws, combined with the amplification of patriarchy as a catch-all explanation, suggests a manipulation of narrative to prioritize one gender's needs over another's.

Awards
- We have already highlighted how the Government of India applies double standards

in punishing women— they often receive lighter sentences than men for the same crimes, with many escaping accountability by invoking sympathy and portraying themselves as victims or crying Victims of Patriarchy.

- No woman has been executed in India since 1955—even when she has committed murder in ways more brutal than men. Meanwhile, men have been executed for comparatively less severe crimes.
- Law changed for one women murder but more than 600 murders are ignored.
- Women can Inherit husband property even she is accused of his murder. Most of the time Women is convicted for the murder, even she is the mastermind or beneficiary of the murder.
- The Indian Government gives preference to daughters-in-law over a man's parents; under the mandate of the National Commission for Women (NCW), the mother of a man does not fall within their scope of protection.
- Under the mandate of the Ministry of Women and Child Development (WCD), benefits are primarily directed toward the girl child, while boys are not provided the same level of support. Calling it a 'Child Development' ministry is misleading—it would be more accurate to rename it the Ministry of Women and Girl Child Development.

The awards listed above are indirect Trophies due to the government's biased mindset—functioning as indirect bravery awards for women, who are treated in India as an endangered species, while men are routinely ignored. In a country where so-called patriarchy(as per Feminists) prevails, men are expected only to die on the border/battlefield fighting enemies protecting India or pay taxes.

Bias

When systems only recognize one side of the story, they no longer serve justice—they become instruments of institutional discrimination. In the name of empowerment, a dangerous precedent is being set where accountability is gendered and selective. This is not just a legal failure; it is a moral one. The head of the evil is not only the individual who commits the crime but the powerful institutions that enable it through silence, selective advocacy, and biased policy-making.

The truth is in plain sight—now it's up to the reader to judge. Behind many crimes lies political influence, often involving ministers or government backing, Judiciary and Justice system and global policy makers. Women are merely capitalizing on the opportunities created for them, but the real victims, time and again, are men and helpless children.

CHAPTER 13

EVIL BEHIND ATROCITIES

How Institutional Bias Promotes Crimes by Women

In recent years, a disturbing pattern has emerged—crimes committed by women, especially against men and boys, are not only ignored but, in some cases, indirectly encouraged by institutional structures. At the root of this problem lies a deep and systemic bias that starts at the highest levels of governance and global policy-making.

A telling example of this imbalance is the existence of organizations such as **UN Women**, a global body dedicated solely to women's issues. While addressing women's rights is crucial, the glaring absence of a counterpart—**UN Men**—raises serious questions. Why is there no formal international platform to address the rights, safety, and well-being of men and boys? This omission is not accidental; it reflects a deliberate prioritization of one gender's concerns over another's, regardless of changing ground realities.

This bias from the top trickles down. Funding, media narratives, legal reforms, and educational programs are disproportionately directed toward women's causes, often without checks and balances. In such an ecosystem, crimes committed by women—whether it is abuse of legal provisions, false accusations, or even direct harm against men or boys—are often trivialized or dismissed. Worse, in some cases, perpetrators are portrayed as victims themselves, completely inverting the concept of justice.

In recent years, a concerning pattern has emerged: crimes committed by women, particularly against men and boys, often receive less scrutiny and legal consequence. This disparity suggests an institutional bias that originates from the highest levels of global governance.

Institutional Bias in Global Organizations

The establishment of organizations like UN Women, dedicated solely to women's issues, highlights a significant imbalance. The absence of a corresponding UN Men organization raises questions about the equitable representation of men's issues on the global stage. This one-sided focus can inadvertently marginalize the challenges faced by men and boys, leading to policies that may neglect or even disadvantage them.

Legal Disparities and Gender-Biased Laws

In countries like India, certain laws are designed to protect women but lack gender neutrality, leaving men without similar legal safeguards. For instance, the Protection of Women from Domestic Violence Act focuses exclusively on women, not recognizing men as potential victims of domestic violence. This legal framework can result in situations where men have limited recourse against abuse.

Judicial Stereotyping and Its Consequences

The judiciary, tasked with upholding justice impartially, is not immune to gender biases. Judicial stereotyping can lead to preconceived notions about gender roles, influencing decisions and perpetuating systemic discrimination. Such biases can result in the trivialization of crimes committed by women against men, further entrenching inequality within the legal system.

April 2025, The Supreme Court overturned a woman's murder conviction for killing her two daughters, citing a possible temporary mental disorder. The court acknowledged the influence of superstition in rural areas, suggesting she may have been experiencing a mental health crisis misinterpreted as possession by 'invisible powers.' Given the lack of motive and her history, the conviction was reduced to culpable homicide.

Government Bias in Policy Framing: Beti Bachao but No Beta Bachao

India's flagship scheme "Beti Bachao, Beti Padhao" (Save the Daughter, Educate the Daughter) was launched in 2015 with the commendable goal of addressing declining child sex ratios and promoting girls' education. However, what stands out is the complete absence of a corresponding initiative for boys—no "Beta Bachao" scheme, despite rising concerns about issues faced by boys such as school dropouts, child labor, male suicides, and lack of mental health support. This selective policy focus reveals a glaring gender bias in governance, where advocacy and welfare programs are disproportionately tilted toward one gender. True equality cannot be achieved by uplifting one group while ignoring the systemic neglect of another.

When systems only recognize one side of the story, they no longer serve justice—they become instruments of institutional discrimination. In the name of empowerment, a dangerous precedent is being set where accountability is gendered and selective. This is not just a legal failure; it is a moral one. The head of the evil is not only the individual who commits the crime but the powerful institutions that enable it through silence, selective advocacy, and biased policy-making.

Media Influence:

1. Tech Giants and the Echo Chamber of Bias

Beyond this, individuals may attempt to raise awareness on social media platforms controlled by the global tech giants—Google, Facebook (now Meta), Microsoft, and others. However, it's important to understand that these corporations often operate like the tentacles of a larger ideological machinery. Their moderation policies and content algorithms appear to consistently suppress narratives that do not align with a certain worldview, particularly when it comes to issues affecting men.

2. Google's Selective Celebration of Days

Google is known for its vibrant Doodles—custom illustrations and animations that commemorate various global events. They celebrate everything from Women's Day to Dog Day, International Cat Day to obscure food holidays. However, when it comes to International Men's Day (November 19th)—a globally recognized observance aimed at addressing men's issues including mental health, suicide rates, and fatherlessness—Google remains conspicuously silent. There is no Doodle, no acknowledgement, and no support, despite the day being officially observed in over 80 countries.

3. **Facebook's Discriminatory Moderation Against Men's Rights Content**

Try posting a message on Facebook that says "Men's rights are human rights." Chances are, you will receive a warning that your post violates community standards. In many documented cases, users are temporarily banned—placed in what users colloquially call "Facebook Jail"—for several days. If repeated, the platform may even delete your account. In contrast, statements like "Women's rights are human rights" are not only allowed but often promoted and celebrated. This double standard in content moderation reveals an underlying bias that stifles any balanced discourse on gender equality.

4. **Google's Deflection When Men's Issues Are Queried**

Conduct a simple experiment on Google or its AI assistant Gemini. Ask: *"How many husbands are killed by Indian women?"* You'll likely be met with either no direct answer or a redirection to statistics about dowry deaths, which concern female victims. The system refuses to acknowledge or even recognize the possibility that men too can be victims of spousal violence. This form of algorithmic gaslighting dismisses the suffering of male victims and obstructs access to accurate, balanced information.

Just now, I posted similar question on Google/Gemini, and This is the Answer.

*"It appears **you're expressing frustration** about the perceived lack of attention to men's issues by major*

tech companies and the difficulty in discussing men's rights on social media."

Indian Judiciary

Gender Bias in the Indian Judiciary: When Justice Becomes a One-Way Street

India's legal system was founded on the ideals of justice, equality, and fairness. However, when it comes to gender dynamics in criminal law, a worrying pattern has emerged—one that disproportionately punishes men while granting women excessive legal leniency, even in the gravest of circumstances.

Unequal Punishment: Capital Penalty Only for Men?

A glaring disparity is seen in the application of capital punishment. Indian courts overwhelmingly reserve the death penalty for male convicts. Women, even when found guilty of heinous crimes such as murder, rarely receive the same sentence. The judiciary appears to operate on an unspoken belief: that a woman's actions are always rooted in some form of victimhood or desperation, thereby deserving leniency.

In many cases involving spousal homicide, the woman accused of murdering her husband not only escapes the harshest penalties but often continues to benefit financially from his death. Due to existing property and inheritance laws, the accused wife may legally claim her deceased husband's assets, sometimes even while under trial. This creates a perverse incentive structure where the alleged perpetrator stands to gain from the crime.

The Weaponization of Gender-Specific Laws

Over the past two decades, several well-intentioned laws aimed at protecting women from abuse have increasingly been misused as tools of harassment and extortion. Laws such as:

- **Section 498A of the Indian Penal Code** (Cruelty by Husband or Relatives),
- **The Protection of Women from Domestic Violence Act (PWDVA)**,
- **The Dowry Prohibition Act**, and
- **Rape and molestation laws**,

are now frequently cited in cases later found to be either grossly exaggerated or outright fabricated.

For example, numerous women have been documented filing false dowry or domestic violence complaints shortly after marital disputes, often as leverage in property or divorce negotiations. Others have accused men of sexual assault in cases where there was either consensual contact or, astonishingly, no interaction at all. In one bizarre yet real case, a woman filed a rape case against a man, claiming the assault occurred in her dream—and still, the police were compelled to register a First Information Report (FIR).

No Accountability for False Allegations

The Indian Supreme Court itself has acknowledged the rampant abuse of these legal provisions. In several rulings, the Court has referred to the filing of false cases by women as an **"abuse of the process of law."** In one such judgment, it criticized the tendency of some complainants to name nearly every member of the husband's family in complaints—often including people they had never met or lived with—as a form of psychological and legal warfare.

Yet, despite these strong observations from the highest judicial authority, almost no action is taken against women who file false cases. No penalties, no prosecutions for perjury, no legal consequences. This lack of accountability not only violates the principle of equal justice but also emboldens others to misuse the system.

A System That Enables, Not Deters

The current legal climate enables many women to harass, defame, or financially ruin men with little fear of retribution. In extreme cases, this legal shield becomes a weapon, used even to murder or drive men to suicide, knowing that the judiciary is unlikely to impose the same scrutiny or punishment on a female accused.

This unchecked bias undermines the credibility of real victims—both men and women—and shakes public faith in the integrity of the legal system.

CHAPTER 14

VICTIM OR VILLIAN?

Our goal is not to portray all women as criminals, nor do we claim that all men are saints or victims. Crime does not have a gender, and justice should never be guided by it. The law and its punishments must apply equally to everyone, without bias or favoritism. What we seek to highlight—through the examples provided below—is that women, too, can be capable of acts far more deadly, manipulative, and cruel than often acknowledged. In fact, history and real-life incidents reveal that when driven by malice, personal gain, or ideology, some women have inflicted immense harm. A true woman, especially a mother, does not harm her own children by nature; it is only when influenced by toxic ideologies—often propagated under the banner of modern feminist extremism— that such unnatural behavior emerges. Our intent is not to generalize, but to present a reality often ignored: that justice must be based on actions, not assumptions about gender.

The Judgment of King Solomon

Two women came before King Solomon, both claiming to be the mother of the same baby boy.

They lived in the same house, and both had recently given birth. One night, one of the women accidentally rolled over her baby in her sleep, and he died. She then switched her dead child with the living one belonging to the other woman. When the second woman awoke, she discovered the dead baby beside her, but realized it wasn't hers.

They argued before the king, each insisting the living baby was hers.

King Solomon listened carefully. Then, he called for a sword.

He said, "Cut the living child in two and give half to each woman."

At this, the real mother cried out in anguish, ***"Please, my lord, give her the living baby! Don't kill him!"***

But the other woman said, "Neither I nor you shall have him. Cut him in two!"

Solomon then declared, "Do not kill the child. Give him to the woman who wanted to save him. She is his true mother."

Moral and Legacy

Solomon's judgment demonstrated profound wisdom: he used a test of love and selflessness to uncover the truth. The true mother revealed herself not through her words, but through her actions — willing to give up her claim to save her child's life.

Above story is found in the Bible, in the First Book of Kings, chapter 3, verses 16–28.

Modern Indian Women

1) A 26-year-old woman, Mamata, allegedly strangled her two children, Shambu (7) and Shiya (3), to death before attempting suicide on November 21, 2024,

following a dispute with her husband, Sunil Kumar. The incident occurred in Subramanyapura, Bengaluru.

2) In a tragic incident in Telangana's Sangareddy district, a 30-year-old woman named Rajitha allegedly killed her three children—Sai Krishna (12), Madhu Priya (10), and Gautham (8)—to pursue a relationship with her former classmate, Shiva Kumar. According to police reports, Rajitha smothered each child by placing a towel over their nose and mouth until they suffocated. She then feigned illness, claiming that she and her children had fallen sick after consuming curd rice, to mislead her husband and authorities. Investigations revealed that Rajitha and Shiva Kumar had rekindled their acquaintance during a school reunion, which developed into an extramarital affair. Believing her children were obstacles to starting a new life with Shiva, Rajitha allegedly planned and executed the murders.

3) In January 2024, Suchana, the CEO of Bengaluru-based startup, was arrested for allegedly murdering her four-year-old son in Goa. According to reports, Seth checked into a service apartment in Candolim, North Goa, with her son on January 6. Two days later, she departed for Bengaluru in a taxi, carrying a heavy bag. Hotel staff, noticing bloodstains in the room and her son's absence, alerted the police. Authorities intercepted her in Chitradurga, Karnataka, where they discovered the child's body concealed in the bag.

4) Leelawati, aged 32, was sentenced to life imprisonment in September 2024 for smothering her two daughters, aged five years and five months, on February 20, 2018, in Delhi. The court described the act as a "cold-blooded murder" and a "rarest of rare" case, noting the societal expectation of mothers as nurturing figures. The conviction was under murder charges, but the court opted for life imprisonment over the death penalty, citing the well-being of Leelawati's two surviving children (a 7-year-old daughter and a 2-year-old son) and her potential for rehabilitation.

5) In August 2024, Shivani, a 28-year-old woman from Shahdara, Delhi, was apprehended for killing her six-day-old daughter. She confessed to strangling the infant while breastfeeding and throwing the body in a bag onto a neighbor's roof, reportedly because it was her fourth daughter. Shivani initially filed a missing person complaint to mislead police, but the body was discovered, leading to her confession during interrogation.

6) In November 2024, a woman in northwest Delhi's Ashok Vihar was arrested for allegedly strangling her five-year-old daughter, a rape survivor, after her boyfriend rejected the child. The mother took the child to Deep Chand Bandhu Hospital, claiming she was asleep, but medical staff noticed strangulation marks and alerted police. The child had previously been sexually assaulted by a relative in Himachal Pradesh. The mother confessed to the murder.

7) In April 2022, a 26-year-old woman in Delhi allegedly killed her three-month-old daughter. Neighbors reported that her mother-in-law constantly taunted her, claiming the child was not her son's.

8) On April 9, 2024, Gangadevi, a 28-year-old marketing executive, allegedly smothered her two children, Gowtham (9) and her seven-year-old daughter (a sexual abuse survivor), with a pillow while they slept in Jalahalli, Bengaluru. She called the police around 1 a.m. to report trouble at her home and confessed to the killings. Gangadevi, originally from Andhra Pradesh.

9) On April 6, 2021, Sudha, a 26-year-old housekeeping staffer at a tiles shop, allegedly strangled her three-year-old daughter, Vinutha, with a veil and dumped the body at a construction site in Annapoorneshwari Nagar, Bengaluru. The motive stemmed from Sudha's anger that Vinutha frequently sided with her father, Eeranna, during disputes, including a fight over TV channel selection on the day of the incident. Vinutha also reported Sudha's activities and conversations to Eeranna, causing friction.

10) On April 29, 2024, Bhimaneni Padmini Rani, a 59-year-old homemaker, stabbed her 17-year-old daughter, Sahiti Shivapriya, to death with kitchen knives at their home in Shastrinagar, Banashankari, Bengaluru. Sahiti had lied about scoring 95% in her

II PU exams, claiming she failed one subject, but her friend revealed she failed four. So she felt humiliated and confessed, "I couldn't bear the shame. In that moment, I decided to kill her." Rani attempted suicide but survived.

11) In October 2024, Sweety, a 22-year-old domestic help, and her lover, Francis, a 30-year-old call center employee, were arrested for killing Sweety's two sons, Kabila (2 years) and Kabilan (11 months), in Ramanagara, Bengaluru. The children were seen as obstacles to their intimacy, as they would cry and disturb the couple. Kabila was assaulted to death, and Kabilan was strangled. The couple buried the bodies in a graveyard, claiming the children died of health issues. Sweety had left her husband, Shiva, and moved to Ramanagara with Francis. The murders came to light after Shiva searched for his family and locals reported the burials.

12) On June 15, 2024, Ramya, a 35-year-old woman, surrendered to police after killing one of her 3.5-year-old twin daughters, who was severely autistic, in Bengaluru. Ramya had been depressed for months due to the challenges of raising her autistic twins, one mildly and one severely autistic

13) Indrani Mukerjea, a former media tycoon, was arrested in August 2015 for allegedly killing her 25-year-old daughter, Sheena Bora, on April 24, 2012, in Mumbai. Sheena, who worked as an assistant manager for Mumbai Metro One, was abducted, murdered, and her body was burned in Raigad district. Indrani's driver, Shyamvar Pinturam Rai, and her ex-husband, Sanjeev Khanna, were also arrested, with Rai turning approver and testifying that Indrani planned the murder.

14) On February 23, 2025, Mamta, a 46-year-old woman, was arrested for allegedly killing her adult daughter, who was pregnant and unmarried, with assistance from her 17-year-old younger daughter. Mamta assaulted her daughter after she refused to abort the pregnancy, with the younger sister tying the victim's legs to aid the assault. The exact method of killing was not specified, but a case was registered under murder charges. The minor sister, involved in the crime, was not arrested as she was taking her HSC exams.

15) A 22-year-old woman allegedly beat her three-year-old daughter to death in Mumbai. She took the child to Rajawadi Hospital in Ghatkopar, claiming the child had stomach pain, but fled when doctors requested prior treatment records. Examination revealed the child was already dead, with signs of assault. The mother was later arrested in her native place in Bihar.

16)Firdous Ansari, a 23-year-old woman, was arrested in Thane, Mumbai, for allegedly killing her 14-month-old child with the help of the child's stepfather, with whom she was having an extramarital affair.

17) Bharati, along with her boyfriend Vishal, was arrested for killing her three-year-old son, Aniket, in Ambernath, Mumbai. The child was kicked in the stomach, leading to his death, as Bharati was frustrated that Aniket interrupted her time with Vishal. Neighbors reported that Bharati frequently assaulted her son.

18) March 2024, A 25-year-old woman from Raigad district allegedly smothered her two children, aged 5 and 3, as they were perceived obstacles to her plans of marrying her paramour.

19) December 2024, In Chennai, a 31-year-old woman, Divya Ramkumar, allegedly slit the throats of her two children, resulting in the death of her 18-month-old son, while her four-and-a-half-year-old son survived. She then attempted to take her own life but was apprehended and charged with murder.

20) August 2024, A 34-year-old woman in Coimbatore district reportedly threw her two children, aged 9 and 7, into a 70-foot-deep well before ending her own life by jumping into the same well.

21) December 2024, In Cuddalore district, a 24-year-old woman allegedly pushed her two children, aged 5 and 2, into a well before dying by suicide by jumping into the same well.

22) January 2023, A 25-year-old woman in Kallakurichi district allegedly killed her two children, aged 3 and 2, following a domestic dispute. She then attempted suicide multiple times but survived and was subsequently booked on murder charges.

The list is long, and these are not the kind of women we read about in King Solomon's judgment—women who would rather give up their child than see him harmed. These are modern cases where, tragically, some mothers are not only harming or killing their own innocent, helpless children, but also contributing to a system where fathers are routinely denied custody and equal parenting rights. It's a double-edged sword for men: while children suffer, fathers are left powerless and alienated with the blessings from Judiciary and the System.

With this, we proved that women are equally capable of committing the same crimes as men—and at times, even more brutal ones.

With this, we proved that women are capable of brutally killing their own innocent and helpless children.

With this, we proved that women can commit rape, yet society refuses to acknowledge it.

With this, we proved that women often file false cases but escape punishment by playing the victim or claiming self-defence.

With this, we proved that the UN, governments, NGOs, ministries, and ministers support women blindly, without questioning the truth.

With this, we proved that the mainstream media suppresses news about women's atrocities while continuously glorifying them.

With this, we proved that the NCRB fails to collect data on crimes against men, which women-centric ministries use as an excuse to falsely claim that men are never harassed.

With this, we proved that Indian men have no legal provision to record murders committed by wives—unlike dowry death laws—so over 600+ brutal murders are wrongly classified as ordinary homicides instead of spousal killings.

With this, we proved that Indian courts are not punishing those who misuse laws, and in fact, often show sympathy even towards women who commit murder.

With this, we proved that social media censors any news that goes against the agenda of those in control, labelling it "misinformation" even when it exposes real injustices.

And with all this, we proved that the murders of innocent men continue—ignored, unrecorded, and unpunished.

We've exposed all the crimes by *'Bharat Ki Laxmi.'* **Now, readers, it's your turn to judge. A caution to bachelors.**

Contact and Support

Connect with Author:

Need help?

If you know someone who needs support, simply scan the QR code above and reach out to us.

Bibliography/References

- https://zenodo.org/records/4917024 - SILENCING THE TRUTH - STUDY ON MEN.
- https://zenodo.org/records/4537819 - CRIMES BY INDIAN WOMEN.
- https://zenodo.org/records/4537819 - CRIMES BY INDIAN WOMEN: A SILENT EPIDEMIC

Authors Bio

Mr. Rudolph D'Souza, a pioneering family rights activist and one of the Earliest founding figures of the Men's Rights movement in India, has made a groundbreaking contribution through his latest study report. With sharp insights and deep compassion for the unseen victims of the legal system, he brings to light the hidden casualties that are often ignored by mainstream narratives.

He was born in Bombay (now Mumbai) and graduated from Mangalore University. He completed his professional training in computer Technology at IBM, Markham, Canada. In addition to being a legal professional, he is the founder of the NGO **MyNation Hope Foundation**. He has authored several scholarly study reports, one of which has been referenced in a gender studies program by UCLA.

He is deeply passionate about writing. At just 10 years old, he wrote and published a short poem. During his college years, he went on to write and publish 27 short non-fiction and love stories in his father tongue, Konkani.

Through this book, Mr. D'Souza aims to expose and challenge the Toxic feminist agenda that seeks to dominate, control, and destroy a man's finances, mental health, self-esteem, and any chance at happiness. By highlighting false victimhood, he demonstrates that not all women are victims—many are villains too.

Through meticulous research, real-world case studies, and an unflinching look at ground realities, Mr. D'Souza's study serves as a clarion call for urgent reforms. His work urges society, policymakers, and judicial institutions to recognize that justice must be balanced - that in the pursuit of protecting one group, we must not unknowingly destroy another. Only by addressing these silent sufferings can India hope to build a truly fair, equitable, and '**Viksit Bharat**'

Declaration: The author declares that there are no potential conflicts of interest with respect to the research, authorship, and/or publication of this book nor are they affiliated with any Political Parties or Religious organizations. Any resemblance to any person or entity is purely coincidental.

Funding: The author has received no financial support for the research, authorship, and/or publication of this Book. This research study is self-funded by the author.

Disclaimer: This Research study does not used any Fake statistics to justify any views expressed by the authors, Most Statistics used can be found on NCRB, respective Government Ministry websites or on medico legal Journals.